iagnostic

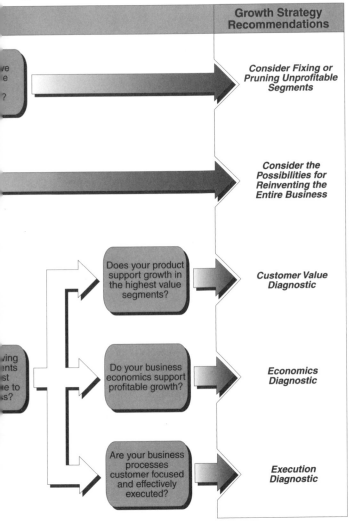

GROW TO BE GREAT

GROW TO BE GREAT

GROW TO BE GREAT

BREAKING THE DOWNSIZING CYCLE

Dwight L. Gertz
João P. A. Baptista

THE FREE PRESS

NEW YORK   LONDON   TORONTO   SYDNEY
TOKYO   SINGAPORE

The Free Press
A Division of Simon & Schuster Inc.
1230 Avenue of the Americas
New York, N.Y. 10020

Printed in the United States of America

printing number
1 2 3 4 5 6 7 8 9 10

Library of Congress Cataloging-in-Publication Data

Gertz, Dwight L.
  Grow to be great: breaking the downsizing cycle / Dwight L.
Gertz, João Baptista.
      p.   cm.
  Includes bibliographical references and index.
  ISBN 0–02–874047–5
    1. Industrial management. 2. Corporations—Growth. 3. Downsizing
of organizations. 4. Strategic planning. 5. Industrial efficiency.
  I. Baptista, João.   II. Title.
  HD31.G437   1995
  658.4—dc20
                                                              95–30558
                                                                CIP

To the management and employees of profitable growth companies who taught us by example.

Contents

Acknowledgments

"**C**orporate Knowledge" and "the Learning Organization" are fashionable terms today. This book is a good illustration of what those terms really mean. Although we must bear personal responsibility for everything that is said here (especially any errors or omissions), *Grow to Be Great* is really an attempt to distill the experience, wisdom, and creativity of 1000 people at Mercer Management Consulting who spend their waking hours thinking about growth and helping companies put those thoughts to work.

In particular, we want to thank those experts on various subjects who patiently educated us on their specialties and then contributed to a series of drafts as the book took shape. We hope that we have managed to convey the full flavor of their expertise:

Chapters 1, 2, and 3 on the importance of growth, which companies really grow and why: Richard Balaban, Rich Christner, Mary Condon, Gregg Dixon, Nate Lentz, Fiona Mellor, Ken Smith, Jason Kellerman and Mike Lovdal

Chapter 4 on customer franchise management: Paul Cole, Randy Dunbar, Lance Hackett, Bruce Onsager, Scott Setrakian, and Bob Wayland

Chapter 5 on new product development: Doug Boike and Mark Deck

Chapter 6 on channels: Bob Atkins and Morgan Chung

Chapter 7 on the foundations of growth: Fred Adair, Eric Almquist, Elisabeth Einaudi, Tom Renda and Robin Tucker

Chapter 8 on getting to growth: Terry Cauthorn, David Gaylin, and James Quella

Throughout the writing of the book, a small and overworked core team kept the process moving. Daniela Pernis-Muldowney functioned as chief of staff. John Wenstrup and Kathy Sun dug up the facts for us. Gregg Dixon maintained and updated a database of 1000 companies. Lauren DeRuisseau and Jane Goodman produced endless revisions of the texts and exhibits. Knowing enough to know what we didn't know, we made extensive use of the services of writing consultant Dick Luecke. A published author in his own right, he knows everything about getting ideas into readable print.

The senior management of our firm, gray from lifetimes of work in the field, provided both moral and financial support. Members of our board Tom Waylett, Jim Down, and Rob Duboff read the manuscript and provided valuable advice.

At the Free Press, Bob Wallace, our editor, was an early supporter and coach who remained tolerant of our most naïve questions while Catherine Wayland and Celia Knight held our hands through the editing and production process.

As the book came closer to completion, we were placed in the unaccustomed position of receiving significant attention from the business press. Pat Pollino and Nick Carr taught us how to deal intelligently with this opportunity.

Finally, and most importantly, we must thank our families for their patience as we pursued this time-consuming venture.

Dwight L. Gertz
João P. A. Baptista

WHAT'S KEEPING CEOS AWAKE AT NIGHT

❉

A great many executives we know are in the grip of a painful contradiction. Their businesses are not growing, profits are under pressure, and shareholders seem to be more demanding than ever. But while their personal circumstances are difficult, the business world seems to be passing them by. The covers of business magazines and the headlines in the press give the impression that nearly everyone else is growing.

This book is a response to concerns that corporate leaders have expressed to us and our colleagues over the past two years. These concerns revolve around the discomfort that executives, as a group, have been experiencing.

The first concern has to do with the value of current strategies for making their companies leaner and meaner. Whether they call it cost cutting or downsizing or restructuring or reengineering, a great many U.S. firms have been actively pursuing strategies to make themselves smaller: fewer employees, fewer operating units, and fewer subsidiaries. In many cases these strategies have been motivated by serious and immediate bottom-line problems. Given slow revenue growth, heavy expenses, and limited time frames within which to improve profitability, cost cutting has been the most obvious solution to anemia at the bottom line. Many CEOs have found themselves saying, "Our shareholders want profit improvement very soon. In the short term, the only solution is to get rid of people and assets."

Of course, not every company that has opted for downsizing has done so in such a knee-jerk or defensive fashion. Some have reduced their costs in well-planned and strategic ways—by simplifying and improving business processes, by shifting resources from unproductive business lines to more promising ones, and so forth. Many have continued these initiatives even as revenues and profits reached record levels. But for every one of these, many others simply began cutting to keep the wolves from the door—at least for a while.

In still other cases, downsizing has taken the place of credible alternatives. As one CEO we know put it: "Every dim-witted idea I see is now dressed up as a growth initiative." These initiatives typically represent $100 million investments with promising *but uncertain* returns. Cost cutting, by contrast, suggests tangible results within a reasonable time frame.

The strategy of shrinkage, however, is running out of steam for many companies. Even when downsizing appears to be paying off and the core processes of the firm have been thoughtfully redesigned, there's always the question of what comes next. Obviously, a company can shrink only so far. There are only so many processes to reengineer, only so many expendable middle managers. A growing number of the executives with whom we have spoken feel that they have already followed these strategies as far as they can go. They find themselves at a strategic dead end. As PepsiCo CEO Wayne Calloway recently told *Fortune* magazine, "You can't save your way to prosperity."[1]

Another common executive concern has to do with shareholder value and its creation. Every CEO knows that "Executive Job One" is creating shareholder value. Indeed, more and more of these corporate leaders are having their interests, through their compensation plans, more closely aligned with shareholder interests. These same CEOs remember that the equation defining shareholder value has a growth factor in it. If they're not growing the business, but simply cutting costs, aren't they failing at Job One? Aren't they maintaining the status quo, but failing to build greater value for their constituents?

The third source of executive angst is personal and emotional. Working for a no-growth company is simply not fun. Executives are reminded of this fact every time they slice the annual budget, and every time they eliminate wage-paying positions. They see many of their best people leaving, and those that stay are only energized by their own fears.

No one is comfortable or fulfilled in this kind of environment. Executives feel good when they can walk into a meeting with analysts or board members and report strong revenue growth. Mid-level managers and supervisors feel good when they know that hard work and dedication today will be rewarded with better and more responsible positions tomorrow. Frontline employees work harder and with greater satisfaction when their efforts contribute to greater security and future well-being.

The different spirits that animate growth and no-growth companies are apparent to everyone. You can almost feel the difference as you walk around their offices and factories. People at growing companies seem to have more fun. They feel and act as if they are changing the world for the better. They spend long hours at work and truly enjoy it. They get positive feedback every time a new breakthrough product hits the market and every time they plan a new facility to build it. This is much different from what we experience in shrinking companies, where friends and colleagues quite suddenly become "nonpersons" and disappear.

Everyone would rather work in an environment where *possibilities* are more tangible than are *limits*—where hope matters more than fear.

Years of downsizing have left companies leaner but not necessarily richer. The result is that growth is the six-letter word on the minds of senior executives and the perceived solution to most of their long-term concerns.

As individual executives articulated these concerns to us, we asked ourselves: How widespread are they? To find the answer, we interviewed chief executives from 180 U.S.-based and 100 European-based corporations. These include many of the largest companies in a wide range of manufacturing and service industries. We found that nearly all the U.S. executives interviewed (94 percent) considered growth a top priority for their companies. Forty-one percent of European executives agreed. Only the issue of global competition (36 percent) came anywhere close to growth as the leading challenge in the eyes of these business leaders.[1]

This book addresses the growth challenge and offers effective steps for breaking out of the downsizing cycle. These steps are built around a framework that identifies proven growth strategies and the organizational competencies essential to their success.

Chapter 1 presents the case. It details the extent to which large U.S. companies are shrinking and presents research indicating why the downsizing strategy is more suited to survival than to prosperity.

Many executives with whom we've spoken believe that the real barriers to growth are self-imposed. Among these self-imposed barriers are a set of myths about growth that, for the most part, represent handy excuses for why companies are not growing: "the economy is lousy," "we're in a dead industry," and so forth. Chapter 2 examines these myths and explains why each fails to hold water.

Our experiences, and the collective experience of our colleagues, confirm that those companies that outperform their industries share a set of traits and behaviors. These are spelled out in Chapter 3. We found that growing companies pursue one or more of the following strategies for growth:

- They focus selectively on better-chosen customers, know everything they can know about those customers and their needs, and serve those needs with intense dedication. We call this *customer franchise management*.
- They become exceptionally effective at rapidly developing large numbers of new products that offer superior value to customers. This is a *new products/services development strategy*.
- They find and develop the most effective ways to connect customer segments with their products and services. This is the strategy of *channel management*.

This short list of strategies is not exclusive. But it does represent what we believe to be pathways to profitable growth that are suitable for a great many companies in any number of industries.

Introduction

While strategies are important they cannot deliver their full potential without certain organizational capabilities. Companies that have successfully implemented these strategies have only done so because they have developed certain capabilities—what we call "foundations for growth."

Chapters 4, 5, and 6 explain the strategies in detail, using highly successful companies as examples. We will show how USAA, arguably one of the most successful financial services companies in America, has managed year-over-year revenue growth in a static market by developing an intense relationship with its customer base. Hewlett-Packard is another company that provides valuable lessons in new products strategy. Gillette has grown its revenues from $3.6 billion to $5.4 billion in just five years, with its success based on remarkable product development skills. In the channels management strategy area we profile Staples, whose rising fortunes are closely tied to its innovative office products supermarket. Dell Computer is another case that demonstrates the power of carving out and managing the most effective channels between company and customer.

Chapter 7 explains the *foundations* for growth: a superior value proposition, superior economics across the value chain, and consistently superior execution. No matter what strategy a company uses to pursue growth, these are absolute requirements for success.

Many companies are featured in this book. All are examples of the best practices in one or more of the growth strategies or the growth foundations. In terms of business performance, almost all of these companies fall within the top quartile of U.S. firms. For the vast majority of readers whose companies do not enjoy this level of performance, Chapter 8 describes what they can do to get their firms growing again.

The odds against pulling a company out of a downward spiral are daunting. Even for companies stuck in neutral, getting onto a pathway to growth is extremely challenging. This chapter presents studies of four companies that have faced such a challenge. Appropriate lessons are drawn for general application by readers.

Appendix A will help you to diagnose your own company and to find the factors that impede growth. Appendix B is a list of the large companies—the profitable growers—that were the primary focus of our research.

Although the problems of growth may cause an executive to lose sleep, they are not intractable. The examples given in this book should convince you that the mechanisms for creating business growth may be hard, but they are not mysterious. Any company, in any industry, can put them to work and *grow to be great*.

1

YOU CANNOT SHRINK TO
GREATNESS

✳

America's great corporations have been on a size reduction regimen for over a decade. Downsizing, "rightsizing," restructuring, and reengineering are very different terms that collectively describe this great corporate shrinking act. To their advocates, these are surgical tools for reshaping bloated and inefficient organizations. In the right hands and in the right situations these tools have been effective in improving business performance. Misused, however, these represent little more than analytical excuses for wholesale unemployment.

The downsizing of American corporations, one of the economic landmarks of the 1980s and 1990s, has had profound implications for the middle class, and has left no group of employees untouched. It has spread beyond the traditional class of victims—blue-collar and lower-level clerical workers—to the ranks of managers and technical professionals. According to a 1987 study by the Conference Board, U.S. corporations eliminated more than a million managers and professional staff positions between 1979 and 1987. And the impulse to shrink corporate headcounts among these employee categories continues unabated.

Some of the biggest companies have been the biggest shedders of personnel. Between 1982 and 1992, General Electric reduced its work force by 25 percent, or 100,000 employees. In 1993–1994, NCR cut 21,500 positions. Atlantic Richfield began the 1980s with a work force of 50,000; less than half of that number remains with the firm today. Sears, Kodak, and Procter & Gamble were also among the shrinking giants of the early 1990s, accounting for well over 73,000 lost positions—many in the managerial ranks. Taken together, the Fortune 500 industrial companies managed to shed 2.6 million jobs between 1984 and the end of 1993. Even among Fortune 500 service companies, current employment has shrunk to 1989 levels.

In general, the huge work force cuts in American corporations have not been tied to performance in the overall economy. In fact, some of the biggest force reductions have coincided with a period of national economic growth. Everyone expects big personnel cuts during hard times, and the recession of 1990–1992 proved to be no exception. Some 1.6 million jobs were lost during that period. But according to a recent American Management Association (AMA) study, as little as one-third of these employment reductions can be attributed solely to general business conditions.[1] Some other factor has been at work, eliminating positions on a permanent basis. The pattern of restaffing that normally follows a recession did not occur once the economic engines of the country regained their momentum. America's big corporations didn't hire many people back, in part because a large percentage of the original layoffs—an estimated 680,000—were attributable to corporate downsizing. Fewer positions needed to be refilled once the recession ended. Many corporations, in fact, just kept on cutting as the economic recovery surged forward in 1993–1994.

A BRIEF HISTORY OF CORPORATE SHRINKAGE

Downsizing was a response to a situation that faced many major U.S. corporations. In general, the first companies to begin the process of downsizing were those hit by direct foreign competition in the late 1970s: companies in steel, machine tools, automobiles, and electronics. These firms recognized that they had massive cost disadvantages, primarily in comparison with their Japanese competitors. Automakers, for example, discovered that they had roughly a $1,000 per vehicle cost disadvantage when compared to Japanese vehicles in the small-car category. Only a small part of this startling difference was traceable to direct labor, the traditional whipping boy for U.S. cost problems. The bulk of the difference was embedded in other cost structures of the corporation, in particular, the number of middle managers and engineers throughout the company. Sheer survival for Chrysler and other industrial companies required massive reductions in the number of "suits" on the payroll.

American steel was another industry to feel the heat during the late 1970s and early 1980s. Companies saw their profit margins evaporating and jumped to the conclusion that foreign competitors, chiefly in Japan, were dumping steel onto the U.S. market at less than their own costs of production. Studies of Japanese steel-making costs, however, pointed to a different conclusion. The Japanese were actually making a *profit* on their U.S. sales. They enjoyed such favorable cost structures that they could sell beneath the prices of U.S. competitors and still enjoy healthy margins. Big Steel found itself squeezed as well by domestic rivals like Nucor, which had made tremendous innovations in the production of steel.

The wave of Japanese competition that began in the 1970s did not confine itself to heavy manufacturing but spread to other sectors where U.S. firms supposedly enjoyed important advantages in technology and innovation. Xerox Corporation, which had dominated the market for photocopying machines, found itself in a similar cost predicament. In 1981, Xerox discovered that machines offered by Minolta, Ricoh, Canon, Toshiba, and other Japanese firms were selling at prices that were less than Xerox's own cost of production![2] And the new Japanese machines offered equal or greater quality and reliability. Three years later, William F. Glavin, then Xerox executive vice president, summarized his company's problems in a statement that described the cost problems of many American companies at the time: "Our manufacturing facilities were highly labor intensive. We built up a huge overhead structure of indirect white-collar workers. Our organization was bogged down with far too many checks and balances."[3]

Clearly, the behemoths of U.S. industry would have to get lean and mean if they hoped to compete and maintain leadership in the future. Xerox's response was thoughtful and effective. Through its partner, Fuji-Xerox, it learned and adopted Japanese principles of quality management and product design that had given Japanese companies such a cost and quality advantage. Other U.S. firms in electronics, autos, and other industries followed a similar course, bringing costs and quality into line with the wave of tough new competition sweeping their markets.

At the same time, these companies sought ways to eliminate layers of bureaucracy and management. Some did it for all the right reasons: too many layers added to costs, slowed the pace of decision making, and isolated decision makers from both customers and their own line workers. Others companies simply took a broad-ax approach to eliminating employees.

Freight rail is another example of a stagnant and bloated industry in which downsizing, restructuring, and reengineering were long overdue. Until 1980, rail companies were kept at inefficient levels of staffing by a century of government regulation and labor agreements that thwarted technological advancement, even as truckers were stripping rail transport of the most attractive segments of the freight business.

Deregulation during the 1980s changed this situation abruptly, with the result that massive layoffs swept away more than half of all employment in the industry. Thanks to these various downsizing and reengineering efforts, the freight rail industry is experiencing a renaissance, gaining market share once lost to the trucking industry.

For other companies, the imperative to downsize has been driven by a simple fact: their product markets are shrinking and there are no new products to create growth. Consider the plight of thousands of U.S. defense contractors. With the Cold War now behind us, the market for most defense-related products is declining on a year-to-year basis. If you're in the business of building nuclear submarines, you must either develop new product markets and/or downsize the company as your backlog of orders dries up.

In general, the drive to reduce costs and gain operating efficiencies has taken these directions:

- *Consolidation of operations.* This is the usual outcome in the case of major acquisitions. Entire departments and production facilities become redundant. Eliminating people, particularly nonunionized, white-collar workers, is usually the quickest and easiest cost-saving step.

- *Sale or elimination of noncritical units.*
- *Using fewer assets.* Just-in-time methods make it possible to reduce inventories and the people who handle them. In a related sense, financial managers have found ways to reduce the amount of working capital needed to operate the companies. Redesign of products and processes leads to lower raw material requirements and fewer assembly steps.
- *Reengineer key processes.* Because the goal of reengineering is to improve the ratio of work output to work input, most companies that adopt this improvement methodology eliminate workers. In a 1994 study by CSC Index, 73 percent of U.S. and 84 percent of European companies responded that reengineering would eliminate jobs, typically by about 21 percent.[4] The same study notes that although reengineering can be used for both cost reduction *and* revenue growth, "to date, it appears, it has been used more to cut costs (and often people)."[5]

LIMITATIONS OF DOWNSIZING

On the surface, a strategy of downsizing to achieve operational efficiencies seems eminently logical. After all, a company that is more efficient than its competitors can either reap higher profit margins or underprice them to win greater market share. Unfortunately, none of the business improvement skills that make it possible to become the lowest-cost, most responsive, highest-quality producer are proprietary. These skills can be learned and applied by just about any company anywhere in the world. Japanese firms discovered this to their regret as one American company after another adopted just-in-time and total quality programs. U.S. automakers sought the advice of the same quality experts who had taught the principles of quality management to their Japanese competitors.

Over time, American firms closed the quality and cost gaps that had made their products less desirable than foreign models. But these pioneers of business improvement soon found that their

domestic competitors could do the same. This was a game that anyone could play. The result is that cost and quality have become
moving targets. Quality has continued to rise and costs have continued to fall, creating a kind of treadmill for many companies.

A strategy of downsizing is also limited by the fact that it may
not address the fundamental problem in a particular business.
Costs, after all, are not the only business problem. For some companies, the problem is not *how* they do things but *what* they do. If
you had been the CEO of a phonograph record manufacturer not
so many years ago, you would have discovered that no amount of
cost reduction or effectiveness gained through reengineering
would have kept your company afloat. Demand for vinyl records—
at any price—simply disappeared. Companies in this situation need
"reinvention" more than they need restructuring or reengineering.
They need to offer entirely new products or services that build on
their historic strengths.

Given these limitations, there is every reason to theorize that
downsizing may be a strategy whose time has passed.

THE DIMINISHING VALUE OF DOWNSIZING

Fortunately, we do not have to rely on theory to infer the long-
term results of downsizing and other cost-cutting strategies. So
many companies have adopted these strategies that we can observe
the outcomes directly. Since 1988, the American Management
Association has been surveying the work force reductions of its
members. Concentrated on larger firms (over $10 million in rev-
enues) and on manufacturing companies, the AMA's studies give us
a picture of what is going on and why.

According to an AMA survey released in 1993, fewer than half
(45 percent) of downsizing companies reported an increase in
operating profits (see Figure 1–1). Almost the same percentage of
firms experienced either no change or an actual decline in operating profits after downsizing.

Since most of these initiatives were motivated by the need to
boost operating profits, these results can only be viewed as dis-

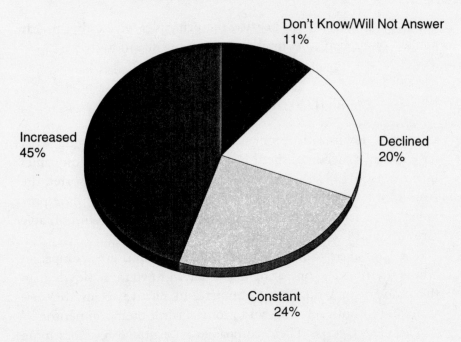

Figure 1–1. Downsizing and Change in Operating Profits
Source: American Management Association, *1993 Survey on Downsizing.*

couraging. Worse still, two-thirds of the downsizing companies have gone back for two or more rounds of work force reductions. Clearly, the cost reduction impulse can be addictive and executives need continuing "quick fixes" to bolster their bottom lines.

Every downsizing initiative, of course, leaves a smaller organization from which to extract the next round of cost savings. Over subsequent rounds, cost cutting must have diminishing returns. In this sense, downsizing is only a short-term fix with limited value to an organization. Corporate anorexia is not a sensible way to get healthy.

Evidence is also growing that downsizing is an uncertain strategy. In fact, a study by CSC Index indicates that fewer than one-third of process reengineering initiatives met or exceeded their goals. Admittedly, similar poor results could be cited for business improvement schemes of the past, including matrix management and total quality management. This is not to condemn the principles behind these improvement plans, which are often sound. In most cases, failure results because the principles were either poorly applied or applied to inappropriate business situations.

THE SHAREHOLDERS' VIEW

Driven to downsize in order to maintain shareholder value, what have managers accomplished? Using the Fortune 1000* companies in the period 1988 through 1993 as a sample, we have sorted the American business world into four groups to which we have provided shorthand names: Shrinkers, Cost Cutters, Unprofitable Growers, and Profitable Growers.

The Shrinkers. Shrinkers, by our definition, are companies whose revenues *and* operating profits have grown more slowly than the industry in which they compete. In relative terms they are shrinking in both revenues and profits against their competitors.

The Cost Cutters. These companies have grown revenues more slowly than their industry, but have grown profits more rapidly. The implication is that the profit growth came largely through cost reductions. We would expect to find many of our downsizing and reengineered companies in this group. Cost Cutters create profits for shareholders, but even the most effective Cost Cutters must eventually reach a point where costs are zero percent of sales, at which point they must grow revenues in order to continue the growth of profits.

The Unprofitable Growers. Companies in this group, by contrast, have managed to increase revenues faster than the industries in which they compete, but without commensurate growth in operating profits.

The Profitable Growers. These companies have managed to increase both revenue *and* profits more rapidly than their industry competitors during the period 1988–1993. It is this group of companies from which we draw most of the examples throughout this

---

* Until 1994, the Fortune 1000 was the 500 largest U.S. industrial corporations and a selection by category of 500 large service businesses. In 1994, Fortune eliminated the service/industrial distinction to create a list of the 500 largest firms ranked by revenue, regardless of industry.

book, and it is in this group that every company would like to find itself.

The distribution of Fortune 1000 companies within this typology of firms is represented in Figure 1–2. Note how wide the distribution is. There are some dramatic winners and losers from which we should be able to learn.

The stock market values these company types very differently. In a recent study of nearly 1,000 large U.S. companies, we found clear evidence that, as far as the stock market is concerned, a penny saved is not as valuable as a penny earned (Figure 1–3). Investors place a much higher value on companies that improved their bottom lines through revenue growth than through cost cutting. From 1988 through 1993, the compound annual growth rate in the market value of these "Profitable Growers" was 19 percent. Over that same period, the companies that achieved higher-than-average operating profit growth but lower-than-average revenue growth—the "Cost Cutters"—saw their market value grow only 12 percent annually. Profitable growth, in other words, was rewarded much more richly than effective cost-cutting. The "Unprofitable Growers" are further behind in the pack at 8 percent, and "Shrinkers" are at the bottom with 5 percent.

The reason for this clear preference for profitable revenue growth may be a recognition on the part of investors that gains made through cost cutting represent either a single event or one that can only be repeated a limited number of times. Eventually, cost cutters run out of fat to trim and competitors can often match their cost reductions, leaving the original cost cutters in the same market position. But enterprises that generate new profits from growing revenues are building a *profit machine* capable of generating a future stream of profits. In the final analysis, it is that future stream of profits that investors are paying for.

This willingness to pay for future profits also manifests itself in the price that the securities markets charge for capital. As Figure 1–4 shows, Profitable Growers are much more likely to earn the cost of capital. Many financial theorists believe that long-term corporate survival depends on the ability to earn returns higher than the cost of capital that the market charges for debt and equity capital.

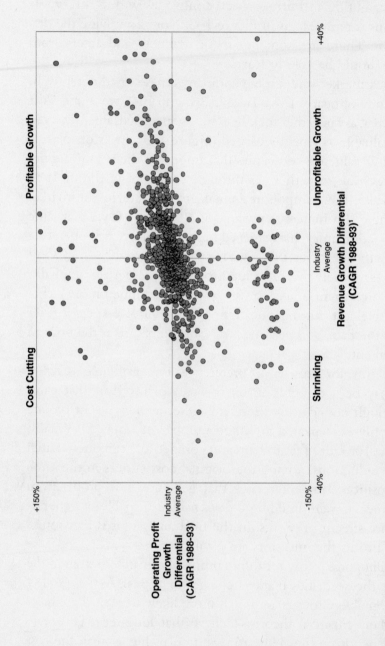

Figure 1–2. Operating Income and Revenue Growth (Fortune 1000 Companies 1988–1993)

[1]Two percent of sample size lies outside of graph range.

Source: Compact Disclosure, Mercer Management Consulting analysis.

Note: Growth rates based upon nominal changes in revenues and operating income.

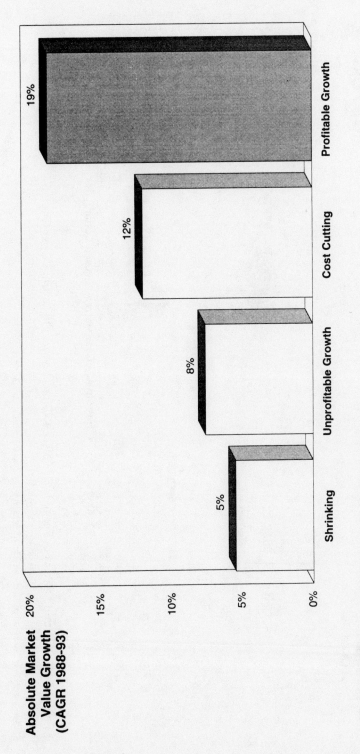

Figure 1–3. Effect of Growth on Shareholder Value

Source: Valueline, Mercer Management Consulting analysis.

17

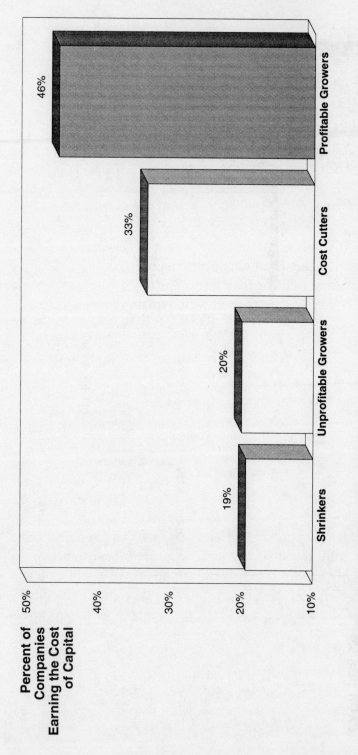

Percent of Companies Earning the Cost of Capital

- Shrinkers: 19%
- Unprofitable Growers: 20%
- Cost Cutters: 33%
- Profitable Growers: 46%

Figure 1–4. Profitable Growers Earned the Cost of Capital More Often than Cost Cutters

Source: Mercer Management Consulting analysis.

Note: n = 572 companies. Uses weighted return on capital for the period 1990–1993.

MORALE AND PRODUCTIVITY

In addition to the quantifiable benefit of being a Profitable Grower instead of a Cost Cutter, there are other benefits that we believe are equally important but harder to measure: morale and productivity.

It is easy to believe that an organization whose employees are systematically reduced in number will have low morale. The people left behind generally remain at their posts with a sense of impending doom, knowing that they could be the next to go and that no one's job is truly safe. One company's experience makes the point clear. In describing the ongoing head count reductions at Scott Paper in the summer of 1994, *New York Times* reporter Glen Collins wrote: "Many Scott employees are in a state of shock, dread and anger as they wait for their managers to decide who will go and who will stay."[6] Many of those who remain end up picking up part of the work left behind by furloughed colleagues—often with no added pay.

A 1994 study of more than 4,000 American workers conducted by Wyatt Co. found that only 57 percent of workers in downsizing companies were generally satisfied with their work, as opposed to 72 percent in growing companies. How this sense of siege among employees translates into costs for the company is easy to understand, and evidence makes clear what we all know intuitively: that in an age when knowledge, know-how, and human ingenuity are more important than capital and physical labor, it doesn't pay to demoralize workers.

The rumors, gossip, and lifeboat mentality that prevail in most downsizing and restructuring situations are not conducive to morale or productivity. Not surprisingly, the AMA study indicates that 80 percent of downsizing companies experienced downturns in morale. "The surest after-effect," it found, "is declining work force morale, which affects productivity and, in turn, profits."[7] The survey indicates that only one-third of the downsized companies experienced increased employee productivity.

To their credit, a great number of firms attempt to soften the blow of work force reduction. Often those with the greatest length of service to the company are protected, and gradual reductions through attrition are common. Ironically, these well-meaning policies may be damaging in the long run, resulting in an aging work force and hiring freezes that bar the door to young, energetic, and newly trained personnel. This is particularly worrisome to technology firms that rely on fresh blood to keep themselves on the leading edge of their markets.

There is also mounting evidence that managers who remain with downsizing companies may be very negatively affected by the experience. They are the ones who must deliver the pink slips, and they are the ones who often pick up the work of their departed comrades. Psychologists who have studied these managers often describe them as stressed, morose, more cautious, and fatigued. Some speak of "survivor's sickness," the combination of guilt and depression that often afflicts survivors of plane crashes and military combat. Yet these managers are the very core employees upon whom downsized companies depend for leadership and creative solutions.

MANAGERIAL TUNNEL VISION

Despite all that has happened, many companies believe that they are poised for growth—even those whose performance over the past several years has been disappointing. Important segments of U.S. business have taken their medicine; they have improved quality and cycle times, and have narrowed or eliminated cost differentials with foreign competitors. Today, the cost of producing a ton of steel or a personal computer or any number of other products and services has been dramatically reduced. Unit labor costs in American industry fell by an average of 6.4 percent a year during the period 1985–1993. Where downsizing has not yet taken hold, as in Germany and Japan, these same cost measures have increased—by 4.2 percent per year in Germany and 6.6 percent in Japan, as reported in *The Economist*.[8]

But even for companies that have gained these efficiencies and swept away unproductive layers of bureaucracy and management, growth will not be automatic. There remains a barrenness of outlook as to what should come next. While business improvements of the 1970s and 1980s may have ensured their survival, they have done little to ensure prosperity. At the same time, 15 years of attention to continuous improvement, quality control, and reductions in staffing and cost have fostered managerial tunnel vision. This condition rivets executive thinking and energy on ways of gaining efficiencies in existing businesses while obscuring their vision of new possibilities for future growth.

Almost an entire generation of managers has adapted itself to the challenge of making companies smaller and *more efficient at what they do.* This has made them less able to *envision what they must become.* In a sense, these managers have become skilled in methodologies that ensure near-term survival, but few have gained experience in the skills that lead to a prosperous future.

It is difficult, though, to fault managers in this. Survival always comes first, and survival has been a central managerial challenge in American business for the past 15 years. Still, the challenge of today and tomorrow is growth, and growth requires a different mind-set and a different set of skills. Many CEOs with whom we have worked are keenly aware of this problem and wonder openly if their managers would know what to do with a growth opportunity if one should come their way.

We believe that these managers can break out of the cycle of downsizing and move their companies toward growth. This book contains examples of managers who have, and it explains the strategies and organizational capabilities that have made growth profitable.

2

SHATTERING THE MYTHS OF CORPORATE GROWTH

✻

Up to this point, our observations upon the limits of downsizing and the value of growth are not entirely unique. Indeed, business thinking is now converging on the notion that it is time to change direction and begin to concentrate on growth. This, unfortunately, could lead to a lot of misdirected energy. We believe that a necessary first step in setting an appropriate growth course is to clear away a number of popular myths, because believing the wrong things can lead to taking the wrong actions.

MYTH #1: GROWTH IS COMMON

From what we read and hear, we may be led to conclude that most companies are growing while a few "problem" companies are not. Actually, profitable growth is very difficult to achieve. The compound annual revenue growth rate for the Fortune 500 industrial companies between 1983 and 1993, adjusted for inflation, was −0.33 percent. Fortune 500 services companies did somewhat better, at 2.2 percent compared to 2.8 percent for the economy as a whole.

As management consultants, we've seen hundreds of corporate strategic plans, and most of them anticipate real double-digit growth—especially three to five years from now when business conditions will have improved. Given the aggregate figures that have been cited, very few companies are hitting their targets. Figure 2–1 plots the compound annual growth in revenues for the Fortune 1000 companies. As the curved line indicates, very few of

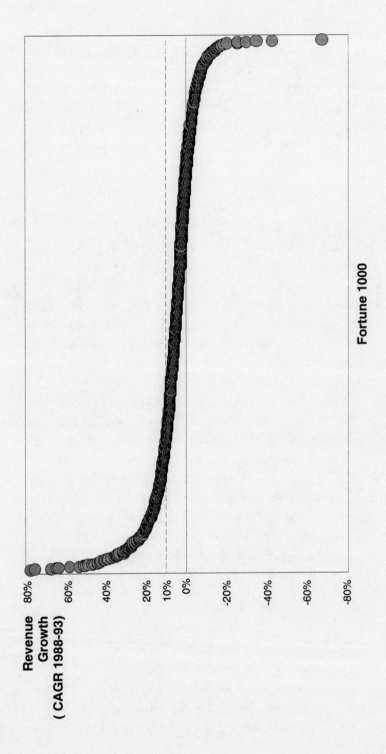

Revenue Growth (CAGR 1988–93)

Fortune 1000

Figure 2–1. Nominal Revenue Growth Rates (1988–1993)

Source: Compact Disclosure, Mercer Management Consulting analysis.

Note: Five companies lie outside the graph range.

these firms actually broke above the line representing 10 percent growth. Only 30 percent did so. Fifty percent failed to expand their revenues at the rate of inflation and GNP growth. In real terms these companies are shrinking, not holding their own in the economy. Nineteen percent failed to achieve even nominal growth.

These figures indicate that real double-digit growth is very difficult to achieve, and that the odds are 2 to 1 against any company reaching it.

MYTH #2: WE ARE ENDING A SHORT AND UNUSUAL PERIOD OF DOWNSIZING— "NORMAL" TIMES ARE AHEAD

One problem with the data we have used to attack myth #1 is that it is taken from the period we have been discussing—the years in which so many large corporations felt compelled to downsize. There was actually a fairly pervasive argument in 1994 that we have felt the pain and will soon all enjoy the gain.

That said, business leaders and business writers are, for some reason, loath to use data to address assertions like this one. So were we, until we began to prepare Figure 2–2. The conclusion over the long term is inescapable. Sales growth, margins, and returns on assets have declined consistently over the last 40 years for Fortune 1000 companies. While focusing on a single business cycle does indeed reveal that a trough will be followed by better times, it does not show that each new peak is lower than the one preceding it.

Managers who are convinced of the value of growth should be aware that they are pursuing a state of affairs that is not only rare, but becoming even rarer.

MYTH #3: IT'S THE ECONOMY

Stockbrokers like to say that a rising tide raises all boats. The idea behind this is that a bull market will lift the prices of stocks in general—even those of lackluster companies. All share in the good times.

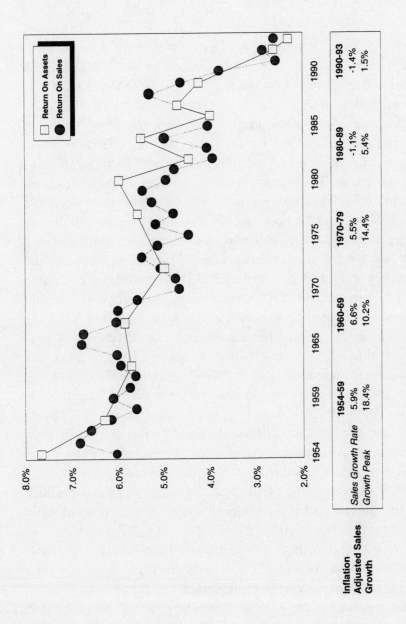

Figure 2–2. Decline in ROA, ROS, and Sales Growth, 1954–1993

Source: *Fortune* magazine (1954–1994), Mercer Management Consulting analysis.

25

Many executives adhere to a similar belief with respect to their company's revenue growth and the buoyant effects of a growing national economy. Sensing a causal link between the progress of the overall economy and the "micro" economy of their own firms, they blame the "macro" economy for their problems and look to periods of economic expansion to fuel company growth. "When things get better," they'll say, "we'll do better." When asked to explain why they have fallen short of the double-digit growth to which most aspire, executives will often pin the blame on "the economy."

It is not difficult to find the source of this rather free association between national economic conditions and the fortunes of individual companies. The financial media bombard us daily with forecasts and analyses of the aggregate economy. The gross domestic product, factory utilization rates, the confidence of purchasing managers, and a host of other aggregated figures are doled out almost willy-nilly on a regular basis. Given this focus on the broader economy, it is easy to forget that for just about every one of us, the national economy is much less important than the smaller economy represented by our own firms and industries.

We believe that a rising gross national product (GNP) will provide limited help to most individual companies. This is because the current average annual rate of real GNP growth is slow, the trend is *downward,* and the difference between good times and bad is less than one might think. From a high-water mark in the 1940s, average real growth in U.S. GNP has declined in almost every decade (see Figure 2–3), and there are no clear signs that this trend will reverse itself in the near future.

The cyclical behavior of the U.S. economy does not produce dramatic upward fluctuations. The difference between good times and bad times is not great when expressed in GNP, which rises to only around 3.5 percent in real terms in a banner year. Even a rising economic tide will not lift corporate fortunes anywhere near the common goal of double-digit growth.

What is true for the United States is proving true for other major economies. Western Europe and Japan have the same patterns of sagging GNP growth. As seen in Figure 2–3, real GNP growth in those economies, though slightly higher than that of the

United States, is still low and trending lower. U.S. companies doing substantial business in these areas should not look to their macro economies to "float their boats" to higher levels of growth.

Notable exceptions to the minor importance of the national economy are certain less-developed countries—Indonesia, Malaysia, and China for example—where periods of double-digit economic growth have occurred and will probably continue. For the long term, companies that aim for sustained growth should be looking very hard at these economies. But for now, they should remember that the absolute level of economic activity in most of these countries remains small—too small to drive the growth strategy of a major multinational firm.

If you harbor any remaining notions that the general economy will do much for company growth, consider this important fact: company growth rates (for both revenues and profits) and broad measures of the economy like GNP are not correlated in any meaningful way. Figure 2–3 tells the tale. Revenue growth for Fortune 1000 companies was broadly scattered over a wide range during a time period in which the growth in real U.S. GNP was around 2 percent.

The conclusion that one can draw from this discussion of GNP and corporate growth is that a rising tide does very little for individual companies over the long haul, and that boats will find their own level.

MYTH #4: BIG COMPANIES CAN'T GROW

America has a tremendous infatuation with "start-up" and entrepreneurial companies. Business literature gushes with inspiring stories of enterprising individuals who, from their basement laboratories or garage workshops, launched companies that grew to become Fortune 1000 players. Many have come to believe that great enterprises can only take root in small organizations unencumbered by the bureaucracies, turf battles, and risk aversion that supposedly characterize large firms. To some extent, this is true.

That said, however, consider Figure 2–4, which plots the growth performance of Fortune 1000 companies against size as measured

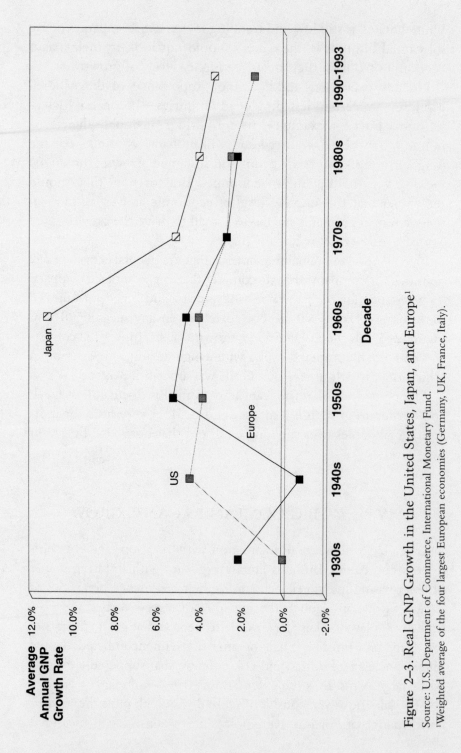

Figure 2–3. Real GNP Growth in the United States, Japan, and Europe[1]

Source: U.S. Department of Commerce, International Monetary Fund.

[1]Weighted average of the four largest European economies (Germany, UK, France, Italy).

by average revenues. Companies plotted on this graph range between $100 million and $100 billion in revenues—a very large spread. Growing companies can be found across this entire range. In fact, analysis of this data indicates virtually *no* correlation between company size and revenue growth rate.[1]

In other words, in the $100 million to $100 billion revenue range, size does not correlate with revenue growth. Thus, the idea that "big companies cannot grow" is yet another myth. To be sure, one can find many phenomenal growth stories among small businesses, and their contribution to the economy should not be underestimated. But the notion that only small companies can grow is as inaccurate as it is prevalent. As Figure 2–4 indicates, companies with revenues of several billions of dollars can be found at either end of the growth spectrum. Wal-Mart, the fourth-largest U.S. company, with annual revenues of more than $82 billion, has posted annual growth of 20 percent in the last five years, and many analysts expect the company to maintain that growth rate for the next five years. Hewlett-Packard, a 57-year-old company with 96,000 employees, thousands of products, and more than $20 billion in annual sales, has quadrupled its size over the past ten years. Motorola, with $17 billion in sales, posted revenue gains of 28 percent from 1992 to 1993 and 17 percent from 1991 to 1992.

Like a number of other large and successful organizations, Hewlett-Packard and Motorola were among the Fortune 1000 companies listed in 1963 and they remain there some 30 years later. This speaks volumes about their ability to generate sustained growth. For example, Hewlett-Packard's revenues grew at an annual compound growth rate of 18.8 percent during this period; Motorola's revenues grew by 13.5 percent.

Size, then, should not be considered an insurmountable obstacle to growth. Even if it were true that substantial growth is easier for smaller companies, the fact remains that most of us still work for large organizations, and if we hope to ensure future prosperity for ourselves, our co-workers, and our shareholders, we must find ways to make these organizations grow and prosper. What propelled the Wal-Marts and the Microsofts of modern business to the major leagues was not, after all, their smallness—it was their entrepreneurial spirit.

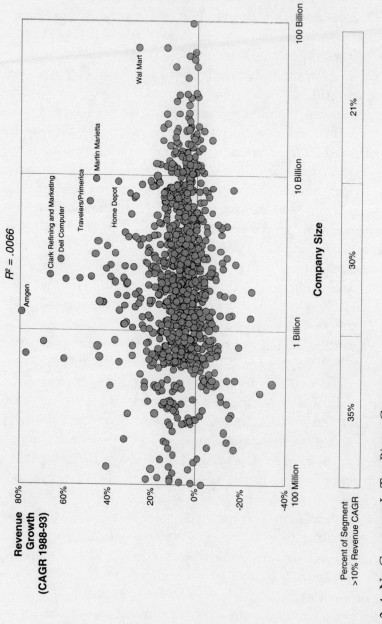

Figure 2–4. No Company Is Too Big to Grow

Source: Fortune 1000, Compact Disclosure, Mercer Management Consulting analysis.

The notion that this spirit is buried by the bureaucracies and politics of large corporations has become conventional wisdom, even though we see plenty of large companies that have maintained their vitality.

In their study of business rejuvenation, British scholars Charles Baden-Fuller and John M. Stopford observed that poorly performing mature companies were generally narrow, defensive, and parochial in their thinking. Their managers held to "linear, top-down, mechanistic views of the world." In contrast, high-performing mature companies were able to maintain the features of entrepreneurial organizations: teamwork, high aspirations, the freedom to experiment, the capability to learn and adapt, and the capacity to recognize and resolve the dilemmas that unfold over time.[2] Research by Zenas Bloch and Ian MacMillan also points to organizational culture—not size—as the key factor in corporate entrepreneurship: "Most large corporations, driven by the need to protect and optimize the use of existing resources, discourage the pursuit of opportunity."[3]

The findings of these scholars confirm the sentiment of the eminent business historian Alfred Chandler, who in *Scale and Scope* likewise rejected the conventional wisdom that associates innovation and economic dynamism with small firms.[4]

MYTH #5: WE'RE IN A DEAD ("NO GROWTH") INDUSTRY

This may be Myth #5, but our experience also suggests that it is Excuse #1. "This is a no-growth industry. How can we be expected to expand revenues and profits?"

Yes, to be sure, it is tough growing in an industry that suffers from overcapacity, declining demand, powerful labor unions, and burdensome regulation. But Figure 2–5 tells another tale.

This figure indicates the range of revenue growth rates for Fortune 1000 companies in 12 major industries. With the exception of pharmaceuticals and computers, none of these would be viewed as a "hot" industry. When was the last time a stockbroker called you with a great story about a company in basic metals, chemicals, or paper? Nevertheless, even within these allegedly mundane industries, some com-

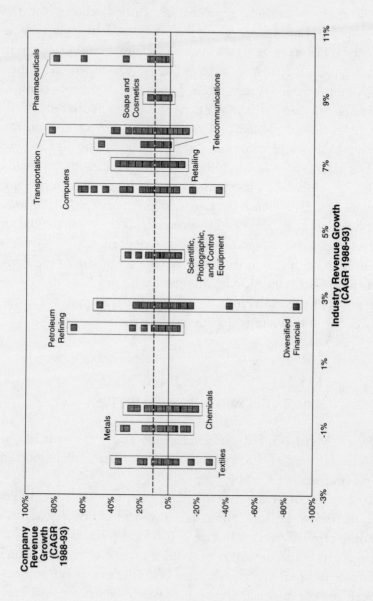

Figure 2–5. Growth Opportunities Exist in Every Industry

Source: Fortune 1000, Compact Disclosure, Mercer Management Consulting analysis.

TABLE 2–1

Growth Leaders by Industry

Industry	Industry Revenue CAGR (88–93)[1]	Industry Leader	Company Revenue CAGR (88–93)
Textiles	–2%	Unifi Inc.	36%
Metals	–1%	Maxxam Inc.	31%
Chemicals	0%	Great Lakes Chemical Corp.	24%
Petroleum Refining	2%	Tosco Corp.	26%
Diversified Financial	3%	Primerica	47%
Scientific, Photographic, Control Equipment	4%	US Surgical Corp.	29%
Computers and Office Equipment	6%	Dell Computer Corp.	62%
Retailing	7%	Home Depot Inc.	36%
Telecommunications	8%	McCaw Cellular Communications Inc.[2]	48%
Transportation	8%	Mesa Airlines Inc.	82%
Soaps and Cosmetics	9%	Safety Kleen Corp.	14%
Pharmaceuticals	10%	Amgen Inc.	81%

[1]Figures rounded to the nearest digit.
[2]Acquired by AT&T after the study time period.

panies are not only doing well, they are recording double-digit growth rates. As master investor Peter Lynch wrote not so long ago, "If it's a choice between investing in a good company in a great industry, or a great company in a lousy industry, I'll take the great company in the lousy industry any day . . . It's the company, stupid."[5]

In fact, the greater variation is between companies *within* industries, rather than among industries themselves. Within a given industry, the range of performance between the fastest-growing and the slowest-growing companies is greater than the range of performance between the fastest- and slowest-growing industries.

In every industry, companies can be found that are growing far faster (as well as far slower) than their industry as a whole. In the chemical industry, where the overall annual growth rate between 1988 and 1993 was less than 2 percent, Great Lakes Chemical grew at more than a 24 percent clip. In the commercial banking industry, MBNA posted revenue gains in excess of 25 percent over this period. When it comes to individual companies, any industry can be a growth industry.

Blaming slow or negative growth on industry maturity or stagnation simply does not explain why even the most moribund industries have a number of firms achieving double-digit growth. Baden-Fuller and Stopford, cited earlier, are among those industry observers who believe that unprofitable industries are typically inhabited by a number of unimaginative firms. They state that such unprofitable industries offer great opportunities for success.[6]

Evidence, in fact, indicates little correlation between the growth rates of individual companies and that of their industry. Statistical analysis by Richard Rumelt has demonstrated that less than 9 percent of a business unit's profitability can be explained by the industry sector it occupies. His conclusions point to a firm's choice of strategy as the single largest determinant of success, accounting for over 46 percent of a firm's profitability.[7] Robert D. Buzzell and Bradley Gale, supporting their research with the PIMS database, prove that very little correlation exists between a company's profitability and the industry growth rate.[8]

More recently Cognetics, an economic research firm, goes so far as to state that between 1989 and 1993 the industries with the largest number of fast-growing firms tended to be aged and moribund. Paper products, chemicals, rubber and plastics, and similar "unglamorous" categories led the list of industries with the most companies that had doubled their revenues.

MYTH #6: MOST LARGE COMPANY GROWTH IS CREATED THROUGH ACQUISITION

This is a yes-and-no myth: yes, in the sense that acquisitions can be the fast road to growth; no, in the sense that it is not always the case, given that the road taken may be full of potholes and potential dead-ends.

Shattering the Myths of Corporate Growth

In studying the impact of acquisitions on growth, we were struck by the wide pattern found among high-growth companies. Some of the top performers, such as Nucor Corporation and MBNA, have grown without benefit of any significant acquisitions. Other excellent performers, like The Travelers, are actually the sum of a series of acquisitions. Among the group of profitable growers we examined, 69 percent of revenue growth was generated internally, with only 31 percent coming through acquisitions.

Clearly, while acquisitions are a way to grow, they are far from being the only way. What's more, for those companies that do pursue growth through acquisitions, the risk of failure is high. The landscape is littered with the remains of acquisitions that failed to deliver anticipated benefits. Michael Porter's study of the acquisitions of 33 prestigious U.S. companies over a period of 36 years revealed that more than half of the unrelated acquisitions were later divested. Another analysis, of acquisitions in the 1980s, showed that 61 percent failed to earn even the cost of the capital required for the investment.[9] This should come as no surprise, since the number of companies with real growth potential that are "acquirable" at a reasonable price is actually quite small. Fewer than one-quarter of acquisitions generate economic value for the buyer, earning back at least the cost of capital required for the investment.[10] The great majority actually destroy value. It is usually the shareholders of the acquired company, not those of the acquirer, who reap benefits from a deal.

One might draw the implication from these dismal reports, as does author Michael Jacobs, that "the ability of general managers to operate a business they did not know more than offset whatever financial synergies that were thought to exist."[11]

The failure of some acquisitions can be traced to poor preacquisition planning—the wrong company was purchased or the price was too high. In many cases, however, the deal was probably sound; it was the postacquisition management that fell short. The way management addresses the myriad issues involved in integrating two firms into a single new entity—issues touching everything from information systems to compensation, from organizational structure to organizational culture—often will determine whether a merger succeeds or fails.

Even when they work from a financial perspective, no acquisitions are "easy." In the immediate aftermath of a deal's consummation, productivity almost always falls, by as much as 50 percent by some measures. Customers are lost in the shuffle. Acquisitions create conflict, confusion, and problems of morale among acquired employees. Many have a "conquered nation" mentality. Sanford I. (Sandy) Weill, one of the most successful acquirers of the past 20 years, recognized this problem when he remarked, "The employees of the acquired company didn't choose to work for us."[12]

The facts indicate that acquired employees have every reason to be apprehensive about their future. In the two years following a merger, an acquired firm will on average suffer a 39 percent rate of management turnover, three times the two-year average for companies not involved in mergers. In the case of hostile takeovers, the average two-year management turnover rate is around 54 percent.

Despite these caveats, well-executed strategic acquisitions can provide powerful market and competitive benefits.

Sandy Weill, currently chairman/CEO of The Travelers—in 1994 a $17.1 billion company offering insurance, consumer finance, and investment services—is one of the most visible practitioners of successful growth through acquisitions. Throughout his career, he has demonstrated how thoughtful acquisitions can be an engine for growth in the hands of able mechanics. His success underscores the fact that acquisitions, like downsizing, provide only short-term benefits. Long-term growth demands that acquirers go beyond deal making and "synergies" to building business strategies aimed at besting competitors and satisfying customers.

At Primerica, one of Weill's successful acquisitions, his managers did what other downsizers were doing: they cut costs through head count reductions, consolidated activities, and eliminated losing or ill-fitting operations. Efficiency in operations was the name of the game. This was where all the easy profits would be found. As one manager remarked, "We're operations people. Our heroes have been those who cut costs, who increase margins, and who run a tight ship. For the most part, our talented people are not marketing people, not new product people, but operations people."[13]

But like downsizing, this strategy of increasing profits through internal efficiency has a limited future. Eventually, the improvements and efficiencies are gained, and what needs fixing is fixed. To continue profit expansion, the acquirer must either look for new targets or do what other successful companies do—find a strategy for offering greater value to customers.

Unlike most deal makers, Weill understood this from the start, and he made sure that the companies he bought were focused in attractive market niches where they had commanding distribution strength and opportunities to develop a customer base through improved products and services. "We can only push efficiencies so far," he said. "We have to develop new products and marketing capabilities."[14]

MYTH #7: COST CUTTING SETS THE STAGE FOR GROWTH

Although there is no theoretical reason why "clearing the decks" won't lead to renewed growth, our research indicates that this doesn't happen very often. Of the profitable growers from 1988 to 1993 that we identified in the Fortune 1000, only 7 percent were cost cutters in the previous five-year period, from 1983 to 1988. The transition from cost cutting to growth is apparently a very difficult one. By contrast, the most likely route to profitable growth in the 1988–93 period was profitable growth in 1983–88.

GETTING BEYOND THE MYTHS

The myths just described are not harmless. To the extent that executives accept them as true, they become springboards for ill-conceived strategies, wasting millions of dollars and untold human energy. Citing a lackluster economy, some executives sit tight, expecting better times to boost their fortunes. Those who think their companies are too big to grow, or are in a stagnant industry, ignore the growth potential within their own ranks in favor of risky acquisitions. The experiences of oil companies in office equipment or department stores, and of steel makers in insurance are prime examples. Likewise, Cabot Corporation spent years pursuing diversification, only to discover after much time and many millions spent that its greatest potential for growth was in its traditional chemicals business. The real danger of these myths is that they create a "things are out of our control" mentality for the managers who internalize them. In reality, there is a great deal that managers can do to chart their company's future.

This chapter has identified what is not true about growth. Subsequent chapters address what *is* true. They will lay out a framework for what executives must do to break the cycle of downsizing and get back to growth.

3

WHAT MOST GROWING COMPANIES HAVE IN COMMON

✳

What is true about the companies that are achieving profitable growth? What are they doing that puts them at the head of the pack? In this chapter, we present a framework that describes strategies and organizational requirements common to growing companies. This transition to useful business advice requires that we choose companies for further study. But which ones?

Earlier in this book we introduced a way of dividing the Fortune 1000 companies into four groups—Shrinkers, Cost Cutters, Unprofitable Growers, and Profitable Growers—based on their revenues and profit growth relative to competitors. This allows us to identify companies that are not only strong performers in an absolute sense, but also competitive winners. Using the same five-year data (1988 through 1993), we've compiled a list of what we call "growth champions." Our list includes the Profitable Growers quadrant of the Fortune 1000 companies, as well as a number of other firms whose records of achievement are undeniable. Some of these companies, like USAA, are not part of the Fortune list because they are not public companies. Others are younger companies that haven't yet reached Fortune 1000 status, but whose capabilities for growth are undeniable and whose successes are filled with valuable lessons. A list of some growth champions can be found in Appendix B.

Only 395 of the Fortune 1000 companies fell in the Profitable Growth category of our analysis. These include companies with household names like Wal-Mart, Corning, and Hewlett-Packard, as well as equally successful but perhaps less well-known firms such as Great Lakes Chemical. The list is a source of fascination to people like us, who make a living by offering advice about how to operate a business. Colleagues who have spent a lifetime analyzing business success and failure have pored over this list for hours, alternately reassured by the presence of known exemplars and puzzled by the appearance of other firms.

Table 3–1 is a sampling of our list of growth champions. It draws attention to some of the companies that will be used as examples in the coming chapters, and reinforces our contention that powerful growth can be generated in any industry. While a company like Amgen exerts its superiority in the fast-growing pharmaceutical

TABLE 3–1

Sample of Profitable Growers by Industry, 1988–1993

Company Name	Industry	Industry Revenue Growth	Company Size Revenue ($mm)	Company Revenue Growth	Company Operating Profit Growth
AT&T	Telecommunications	8%	67,156	14%	25%
Amgen Inc.	Pharmaceuticals	10%	1,373	81%	254%
Corning Inc.	Building Materials and Glass	2%	4,005	14%	19%
Great Lakes Chemical	Chemicals	0%	1,828	24%	36%
Pacificare Health Systems, Inc.	Diversified Services	8%	2,200	39%	90%
Hewlett-Packard Co.	Computers/Office Equipment	6%	20,317	16%	10%
Home Depot Inc.	Retailing	7%	9,239	36%	41%
MBNA Inc.	Commercial Banking	11%	1,214	25%	20%
Nucor Corp.	Metals	-1%	2,254	16%	13%
Walgreens	Retailing	7%	8,295	11%	13%
Wal-Mart Stores Inc.	Retailing	7%	67,345	27%	22%

sector, Nucor Corporation, a steel maker, maintains double-digit growth in an industry that actually shrank during the period of our study. Indeed, Nucor executives explain their success in a presentation entitled "Why Nucor Succeeds in an Industry That Doesn't Do So Well."

Creating lists of exemplary companies is a risky business. Some companies fall from grace with amazing speed. Tom Peters and Robert Waterman were reminded of this fact in the years following publication of their book, *In Search of Excellence*. A great deal of criticism was published about the rapid performance deterioration of the "excellent" companies cited in that book. We can't say with certainty that a number of the growth champions cited in this book for their excellent practices will not end up among the "fallen angels." Successful formulas are noticed and quickly copied by other companies. Winning executives can fall victim to hubris. Tomorrow's technologies can decimate today's market masters. What we can say with certainty, however, is that our list of stellar performers made it to the top in very tough times, and that they offer lessons from which a great deal can be learned. Those lessons will most assuredly outlive the success of the companies themselves.

There is also the risk that some of our champions may have achieved growth at the expense of other important business goals. Are they reinvesting in their assets? Are they developing and retaining the human talent that will carry them forward in the coming years? Are they preparing for the future? Time will tell.

PUTTING GROWTH CHAMPIONS TO THE TEST

When we compiled our list of growth champions we didn't know whether they would pass muster against other measures of current and future business performance. So we tested them against some widely used measures. To our relief, every business metric we examined showed that you needn't fear the consequences of emulating these companies.

In addition to demonstrating the stock price growth we discussed in Chapter 1, these companies also have higher price to earnings ratios than their competitors, indicating that the stock market will pay more for a dollar of earnings generated through profitable competitive growth than for a dollar of earnings generated either through cost cutting or less profitable growth.

We also analyzed our growth companies in terms of more sophisticated measures. One such family of measures is typified by the economic value–added (EVA) and market value–added (MVA) measures popularized by the consulting firm Stern Stewart (Figure 3–1). EVA, simply stated, measures a corporation's ability to generate wealth in excess of the cost of the capital it employs. MVA measures the performance of the corporation over the longer term as an investment, and therefore includes the aggregate expectations of investors for future performance. In the case of both measures, our growth champions are a superior group of companies. They also stand up well against the "value based management" methodology advanced by James McTaggart, Peter Kontes, and Michael Mankins, in that they have a much higher chance of earning their cost of capital than the average company.

In this age of "guru overload," we were unable to resist the temptation to measure the performance of the profitable growth companies against the companies cited in the popular management gospels. Figure 3–2 shows that profitable growth companies hold up very well against the market leaders cited in Treacy and Wiersema's *Discipline of Market Leaders,* Collins and Porras' *Built to Last,* and in Peters and Waterman's *In Search of Excellence.*

In short, we firmly believe that no reasonable test of business performance for large companies will result in a failing grade for the growth champions. We also think that any framework for thinking about business strategy will support an informed admiration for what these companies have accomplished.

But merely knowing that our simple measure of profitable growth is supported by other measures does not confirm that our list of growth champions is useful. Is it truly possible to understand what drives the performance of growing companies? Are there clear patterns that others can adopt—even across industries? Any

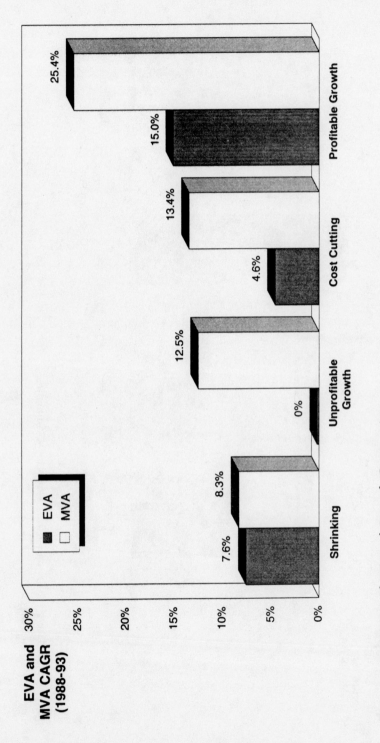

Figure 3–1. EVA and MVA of Growth Companies

Source: Stern Stewart Performance 1000, Mercer Management Consulting analysis.

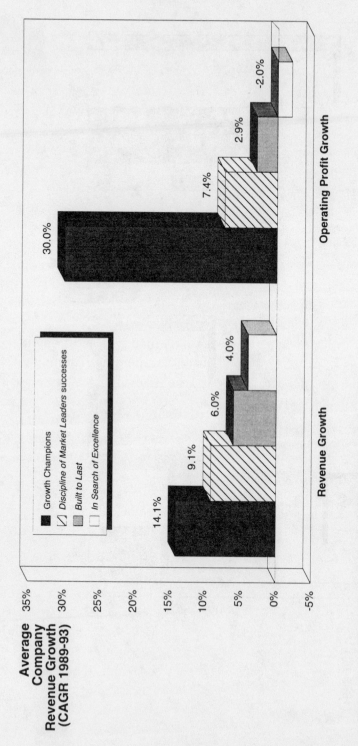

Figure 3–2. Relative Performance of Exemplary Companies
Source: Mercer Management Consulting analysis.

executive who has read about his or her own business in the press knows the pitfalls of trying to understand from the outside what a company is doing or how its management thinks. Even *insiders* disagree about what is going on. In some cases, the management team may even view aspects of its strategy as trade secrets and take extraordinary measures to camouflage the truth.

We recognize these difficulties and that we will never be intimately familiar with all the facts, strategies, and operating methods of every one of our growth companies. We have spoken with representatives of many of them and, with the help of our colleagues, have come to know more and more about these businesses. That process will continue long after the publication of this book.

We continue to expand our research, studying more companies in depth and more countries outside North America. The time period of our growth database is expanding also, both into the past and forward as each passing year adds new data.

With this growing knowledge has come increasing confidence that we can see truly useful patterns emerging. Although each individual company represents unique issues and has a unique story to tell, we have developed some core understandings that can help make sense of the complex issue of growth.

We are confident that we have learned enough to go beyond the myths about growth. The remainder of this book explains what we know to be true about growth companies and how that knowledge can be put to use.

STRATEGIES FOR ACHIEVING GROWTH

From our continuing analysis of profitable growth companies we see two important ways in which these companies can be understood: first, by the strategies they are following, and second, by what they do to make these strategies successful.

Admittedly, every business strategy is unique. There are some broad groupings within our profitable growth group, however, that offer both an explanation for superior performance and useful ideas for managers who want to do better with their own businesses.

Three strategies in particular seem to be followed by large numbers of companies in order to achieve profitable growth against tough odds. These strategies are not mutually exclusive. Companies practice them in a variety of combinations. We have given descriptive shorthand names to each of these strategies.

First, some companies have developed the fine art of *customer franchise management*. These companies have built winning strategies around providing competitively superior customer value to carefully defined groups of customers. This strategy is much more than simply satisfying customers. It requires careful choice of the customer groups that will be served. That choice often produces surprising target groups. Customer franchise management also requires a disciplined approach to serving these customers profitably. The difficulty in properly implementing this strategy can be seen in the fact that there are so few companies that do it well.

A second route followed by a large proportion of profitable growth companies is *superior new product development*. Companies have always recognized the need to be more innovative and to introduce new products and services. There is nothing new in this. The winners who employ this strategy in the 1990s have gone far beyond innovation and creativity, however. They have long since mastered the art of project management for single development projects. These skills are simply the table stakes for playing in today's game. Masters of the new product strategy have the ability to introduce a steady stream of successful new products. Although the challenges of technology and of understanding customer needs remain, these companies have developed management disciplines that allow them to win consistently against competitors with equal technical skills.

A recent study by the New Product Development Association showed that leaders using a new product development strategy are generating up to half of their annual sales from recently introduced products, while lagging competitors in the same fields are generating only 10 percent of sales from new products. With product life cycles shortening, this strategy can be very effective.

The third growth strategy that we identified in our research is *channel management,* which may be the most overlooked approach to improving business performance. Many commonplace products are now sold through channels that didn't even exist five years ago. Entirely new businesses have been built by offering products through channels that established companies had either overlooked or underestimated. For example, Staples, Toys 'Я' Us, and Home Depot have been leaders in the growth of "category killers," a new retail channel in which mass market economics are brought to specialty retailing. Likewise, Starbucks has taken a very traditional product, coffee, and has built an entire business around channels that its highly sophisticated predecessors had not exploited.

Each new channel has its rules for success, and the most aggressive channel competitors are mounting assaults on multiple fronts by employing as many channels as possible. We even found someone selling ice cream by mail, and later we will explain how one company sells cars by phone. The explosion of new channels creates opportunities to attack established competitors and to alter the power relationships within any industry.

If your business isn't growing as you would like, these three strategies can offer promising opportunities. We have devoted an entire chapter of this book to each of the strategies mentioned.

THE FOUNDATIONS OF GROWTH

Not all profitable growth companies follow the strategies just described. Some, for example, sell commodity products to all comers through traditional channels. Others grow through pure financial evaluation of carefully managed acquisitions. But regardless of the strategy employed—and new ones will doubtless be invented—there are permanent requirements for sustained growth. We call these requirements the *foundations of growth*. They are: competitively superior *value* as determined by customers; comparatively superior *economics* across the value chain; and consistently superior strategy *execution* through organizational alignment.

Many companies have excellent strategies but fail to grow because they do not recognize the requirements of these internal

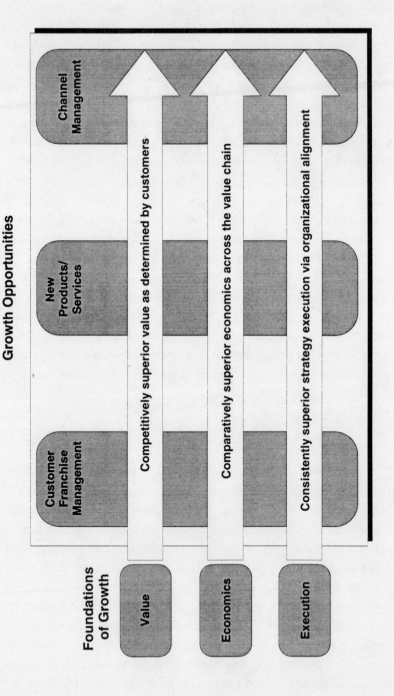

Figure 3–3. Growth Framework

48

foundations. Others may do a good job with one or more of these foundations, but the best growth companies master all three. Chapter 7 explains the precise meaning of each of these terms and makes clear why and how, in any strategy, they are the major determinants of success.

Figure 3–3 portrays our framework for growth, indicating how our three growth strategies (or any others for that matter) will either succeed or fail depending on the degree to which they rest solidly on the foundations of growth.

Our hypothesis is that the three strategies that we have distilled from our analysis of 1990s growth companies, other strategies also currently in use, and strategies yet to be invented can be tested against the tough standards posed by the three foundations of growth. While a failing grade on any of these measures does not ensure failure, it certainly lowers the odds of success.

We also think that the linkages between the three foundations are critical. It does little good to have a spectacular customer value proposition if the series of processes by which that proposition is delivered (i.e., the value chain) is not designed to operate at a reasonable cost. It also does little good to create a space age production and delivery system if the organization cannot make it work.

It is important as well to consider the balance among the three foundations of growth. We have reason to believe that much of the problem with the ever-present fads in business is that they often address a single foundation of growth, leaving the others to somehow take care of themselves. There are exhortations to understand the customer completely, to reengineer the daylights out of the value chain, or to fire up the employees into self-managed teams. In each case, it is taken for granted that everything else will somehow fall into place. It is clear that each of the foundations poses a difficult challenge that must be answered with hard work in its own area and careful coordination with work done elsewhere.

Ask yourself, as you read Chapters 4, 5, and 6, whether you can see the foundations of growth in the stories of high growth companies. In Chapter 7, we will distill these rules into useful tools for the evaluation of any strategy.

4

CUSTOMER FRANCHISE MANAGEMENT

✳

In the early days of the cellular telephone business, competing companies waged war to acquire subscribers. They cast their nets wide, drawing in legions of customers of many descriptions: business people, commuters, techno-junkies, housewives, and even a few drug dealers. Many new subscribers did not stay around long enough for the companies to recoup their acquisition costs. In some cases, the annual drop rate (known as "churn") was 40 to 50 percent. Of those who continued their subscriptions, many were infrequent users and unprofitable to serve.

These early campaigns to gather cellular phone subscribers followed the market share strategy pursued decades earlier by the first issuers of bank credit cards, among others. Capture market share and good things will follow as night follows day. Your costs will fall as the experience curve and economies of scale work in your favor. Becoming the market share leader will make your company the "price setter" that competitors must follow. Profit margins will grow fat and shareholders will be happy.

The fallacy of the market share strategy is the presumption that all customers are created equal: equal in values, in potential profitability, and in responsiveness to marketing initiatives. Further, it requires a product or service offering that is undeniably superior for all customers or segments. Lacking these, the conquest of market terrain can be a costly and potentially Pyrrhic victory. Price cuts, heavy advertising, and sales inducements aimed at capturing customers all reduce margins and sap a company's ability to finance product development, systems improvements, and other means of providing customer value. In the end, the winners of battles over market share often discover that they have conquered territory that isn't worth holding.

Marginal customers are part of the price companies pay when they are blindly driven to increase market share. They find themselves saddled with fickle customers who are difficult to retain and often unprofitable to serve. Investments aimed at building relationships with these customers are often counterproductive.

Fortunately, there are more promising pathways to growth. This chapter explores one of them—the strategy we call customer franchise management. At its heart is the notion that a company can select those customers who are most valuable and responsive to its products and marketing initiatives. Identifying these customers and serving them effectively can be the basis for sustainable business growth.

United Services Automobile Association (USAA), a highly profitable niche player in the financial services industry, serves as a powerful showcase for this strategy. This company demonstrates how dedication to a customer franchise, when combined with product and service value and first-class execution, leads to revenue and profit growth. This combination of strategy, value, and execution has made USAA a $6 billion operation with more than 30 subsidiaries. By 1993, it ranked fifth among U.S. auto insurers and fourth among home insurers. Its compound annual growth rates in assets and profits during the period 1988–1993 were 16 percent and 9 percent, respectively. Not bad for an enterprise that does little national advertising and whose core product—auto insurance—puts it in direct competition with the behemoths of the financial services industry. Its record is doubly impressive considering that its customer base is limited to current and former military officers and their families. This is neither the largest nor the most affluent group of customers, and its numbers are actually shrinking. Nevertheless, USAA's dedication to serving this customer group provides a lesson on the power of customer franchise management.

Meeting members' needs was the whole point of USAA to the small group of army officers that founded it in 1922. Those needs were simple and straightforward: auto insurance for military officers in those days was expensive and difficult to obtain. Most insurers considered them high-risk individuals. Many of these insurers were, themselves, high-risk operations subject to business failure. Also, since auto insurance is regulated by the individual states, frequent transfers meant that military officers and their dependents were continually canceling auto insurance policies in one state and initiating new ones elsewhere. Relationships with old agents had to be dropped and new ones begun with each change of duty station. The time, confusion, and paperwork involved in this process were just some of the penalties paid by military personnel, and which set them apart from the vast majority of American drivers, few of whom relocated across state lines in any given year.

It is not surprising, then, that the one insurer that dedicated itself to their interests would develop a solution. That solution came in two parts. First, because USAA understood the actual risks posed to insurers by military drivers, the company was able to offer insurance at much lower prices. Second, USAA developed a cure for the "transfer blues."

From its inception, USAA has served military officers and their families primarily by mail and by telephone from its San Antonio headquarters. With the exception of claims adjusters and USAA services centers near very large military complexes, it maintains no network of offices, agents, or brokers, instead providing sales and service from this single location. With this centralized organization and one of the industry's most advanced customer information systems, the company has developed a highly efficient system for understanding its customer base and for serving it with competitive products and nearly flawless execution. Together, these give USAA a remarkable competitive advantage and account for a truly enviable record of growth. Today, an Army officer transferred from Fort Benning to Fort Leonard Wood can, with a single phone call, have his or her USAA auto insurance policy canceled in Georgia and reinitiated, at a very attractive rate, in Missouri.

Quick. Convenient. No mistakes. That's one less messy situation for the transferred officer to worry about as he or she changes duty stations. And it's just one of the reasons that nine out of ten officers become USAA members and most stay with the company over long periods, usually long after they return to civilian life.

Customer Franchise Management

Over the decades, USAA has expanded from auto insurance to a broad range of products and services, all aimed at delivering convenience and value to its customer franchise. These products and services are segmented into security (insurance), asset management (financial services), and quality of life (retirement and travel services) products. Today, members can establish a savings account, open an IRA, obtain a credit card, and take out a mortgage loan with USAA's Federal Savings Bank. They can obtain insurance on life and property at competitive rates, and even provide for retirement through a variety of annuities and mutual funds.

When it comes time to purchase a new automobile, USAA members don't have to run around to local dealers and play a game of wits with salesmen. Instead, a toll-free phone call to USAA's Buying Services gives them unbiased pricing information on all makes, models, and options. The Buying Services can finance the purchase, insure the vehicle, and have it delivered to the member. No pressure, no hassles, no hidden charges.

If its members had any doubts that not all insurance companies are the same, the Gulf War was a clear reminder of USAA's special relationship with military officers. Unlike life policies offered elsewhere, USAA policies have no "war clause" that denies payments to people killed in war. When U.S. military forces were ordered to the Persian Gulf in 1990, USAA not only kept the full amount of its members' policies in force, it allowed members to increase their coverage by up to $50,000. The company also set up a Desert Storm Assistance Center to deal with the financial issues caused by the conflict.

Most important, USAA's operating systems and technology make it possible to provide all of these services in a manner that is simple and convenient for the customer and profitable for the company. Members who have had auto accidents report that USAA's San Antonio center can find and discuss relevant documents faster than a neighborhood insurance agent's office.

USAA is clearly succeeding in maximizing its customer assets, and its remarkable rate of growth in the highly competitive field of consumer financial services indicates just how powerful franchise management can be as a tool for growth. *It is better to serve a smaller, less wealthy segment perfectly than a large rich one imperfectly.* Nevertheless, as we'll soon see, the dimensions of customer franchise management extend beyond the example of this single case.

THE CUSTOMER AS THE UNIT OF VALUE

Let's begin with a definition of a customer franchise:

A customer franchise is the portfolio of customer assets with whom a firm enjoys a privileged relationship and for whom the firm dedicates its efforts to create and deliver value.

A strategy based upon the management of a customer franchise is nothing more than a systematic approach to maximizing the value of that portfolio. It requires careful attention to a number of activities:

- Selecting a well-defined group of potentially profitable customers
- Developing a distinctive value proposition that meets those customers' needs better than competitors can
- Focusing marketing resources on acquiring, developing, and retaining profitable customers
- Creating an organization and information system initiating and sustaining profitable relations

This strategy is based upon the *customer as the unit of value*. Not factories, not databases or products, but customers. They are the ultimate asset of any company and the source of its revenues and profits. This is clear from the case of USAA. This company's strength is clearly not the features of its products—its insurance policies, mutual funds, bank services, credit cards, and so forth could be duplicated by its rivals. USAA's strength is its knowledge of its customers' needs and its ability to fulfill these needs efficiently and profitably.

Companies that pursue this strategy may not aim for maximum market share in their industry but instead seek to dominate, as does USAA, their target markets.

Few companies realize the full potential of their existing customers. As a consequence, most have enormous opportunities to grow within their existing customer bases. In many cases, these opportunities are overlooked because of a failure to differentiate between customers who represent real profits and customers who represent only costs. Our analyses have repeatedly found that for many companies, even highly profitable ones, nearly one-third of their customer segments generate no profits, and 30 to 50 percent of marketing and customer service costs are wasted on efforts to acquire, develop, and retain these same customers—money down the drain. Imagine what could be accomplished if these resources were directed toward profitable customers!

To create growth, companies must focus above all else on increasing their customer assets—(1) by acquiring new profitable customers, (2) by developing the profitability of existing customers, (3) by retaining profitable customers and abandoning those that generate losses, or (4) by some combination of these.

Earlier, we cited attempts by cellular phone companies to capture market share. These companies cast their nets broadly, and in the process drew in a great number of customers—profitable and unprofitable alike. Research conducted by our colleagues reveals that the market for cellular phones contains segments with wide revenue disparities. Figure 4–1 indicates the revenues generated by five segments of the cellular phone market. A segment is a grouping of customers with similar characteristics who display similar behavior. In the cellular business five such groups were identified based on the reason customers use cellular phones, the frequency of use, and their ability to pay. For convenience, these groups were called Phone Lite, Budget Class, Techno-Surfers, Mobile Managers, and In-Touch Professionals.

If the costs of acquiring and servicing these different segments are nearly the same, cellular companies should actively try to capture certain customers and not others. They should acquire, develop, and retain those customers who represent the greatest

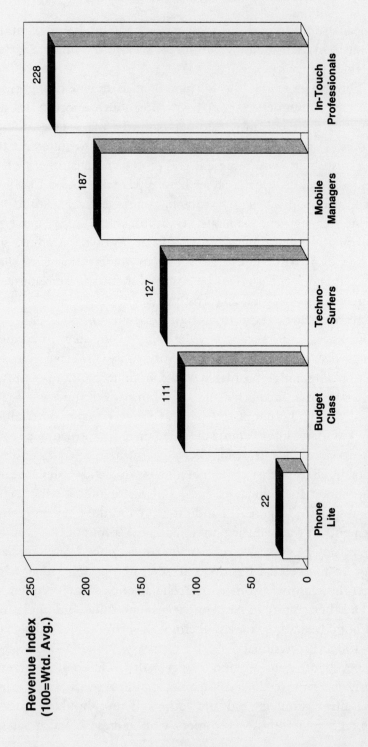

Figure 4–1. Revenues and Cellular Phone Segments
Source: Mercer Management Consulting analysis.

value to the company *over time*. But they can only do this if they have some way of determining a customer's value.

Valuing individual customers and customer segments

In the simplest terms, a customer's value is a function of the costs required to attract and serve that customer and the revenues derived from that customer over time. As productive assets, *customers should be valued in terms of their lifetime value*. Figure 4–2 represents the sources of customer value over time. Initially, this value is negative owing to the cost of acquiring the customer. But with investments in development and retention, the customer's value to the company can grow through a combination of increasing purchases, higher margins, cross-sales, and referrals.

Given the costs and revenues just described, we can use the familiar net present value equation to determine the value of an individual customer. The net present value is the sum of the stream of profits generated by a customer over time, discounted by the firm's cost of capital minus the initial cost of acquiring that customer. Once we know this value, we can differentiate between individual customers (or customer segments), and determine which we should add to our portfolio and which we should leave for our competitors. The concept of net present value also helps us to think through the factors that make the value customer relationships grow. Should we aim at increasing our *margin* or profit per sale? Can we increase sales *volume* with a particular customer or segment? What can we do to reduce the *cost* of acquiring each new customer? How can we increase the *duration* of our relationship with profitable customers? Obviously, the value of the customer relationship is maximized to the extent that these factors can be improved on a cost-effective basis.

In the past, only a few businesses, such as magazines and financial service companies, maintained the data necessary to estimate customer lifetime value. Today, with the increasing application of advanced customer database marketing tools and more sophisti-

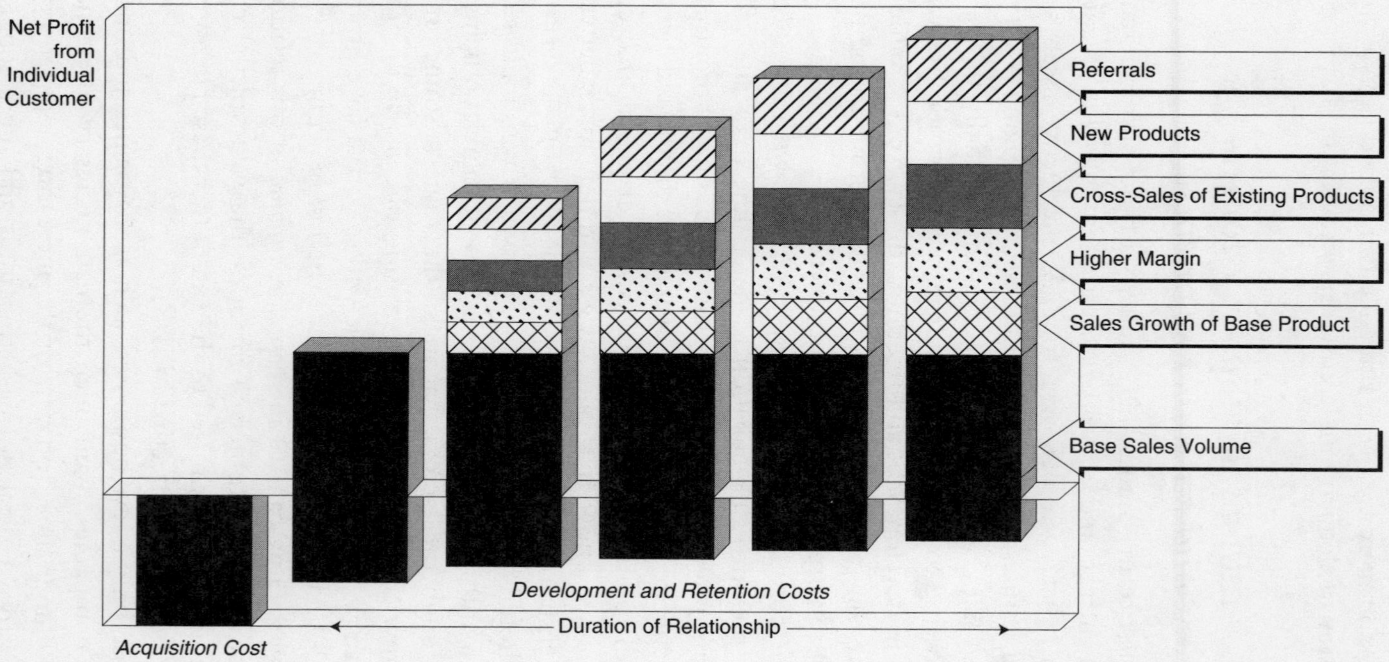
Net Profit from Individual Customer
Referrals
New Products
Cross-Sales of Existing Products
Higher Margin
Sales Growth of Base Product
Base Sales Volume
Development and Retention Costs
Duration of Relationship
Acquisition Cost

Figure 4–2. Sources of Customer Value
Source: Mercer Management Consulting analysis.

cated segmentation techniques, almost any business can develop workable estimates of lifetime values for typical customers within particular groups.

VALUE OF THE CUSTOMER FRANCHISE

If we can estimate the value of an individual customer or customer segment by the method shown above, then we can estimate the value of the entire customer franchise, which is the sum of these individual values.

A typical franchise—or portfolio—includes customers with a wide range of asset values, both positive and negative. When we plot the profitability distribution of customers, we usually find that they sort themselves out in the shape of the familiar bell-shaped curve, as shown in Figure 4–3.

This figure should make it clear why the ability to estimate individual customer or segment value is so important. The typical company, not knowing the asset value of individual customer relationships, views its franchise as a single, undifferentiated bloc. More perceptive competitors identify the best customers, target them, and draw them into their circle. Profits drop as the best customers are picked off. To appreciate the bottom-line impact of these losses, consider a company for which 20 percent of the customers account for 60 percent of the profits—a typical circumstance. The loss of just 10 percent of these high-value customers (2 percent of total customers) can reduce profits by 6 percent! To the extent that the company has fixed costs associated with serving these lost customers, the resulting drop in profits will be significantly higher. It is therefore important to have a clear sense of both the relative value of customers and their susceptibility to switching.

Here are a few of the best measures for tracking the composition of these customer groups within a portfolio:

- The ratio of profitable customers to *all* customers
- The ratio of profitable *new* customers to all new customers

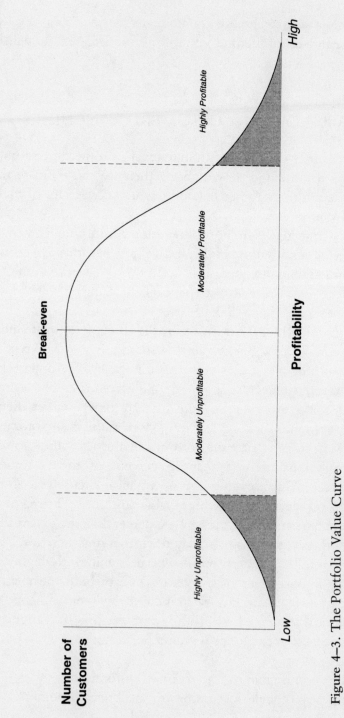

Figure 4–3. The Portfolio Value Curve

Source: Mercer Management Consulting analysis.

- The average tenure of all customers
- The average tenure of profitable customers
- The share of purchases attributable to profitable customers in a particular product/service category

GROWING FRANCHISE VALUE

Companies that pursue the customer franchise strategy manage customer portfolios in ways that optimize their total value. Often, this means working on the "mix" of individual customers or segments so that there are more high-value customers relative to break-even or unprofitable customers.

Consider this hypothetical example. XYZ company finds that its customers fall into four general categories:

- Heavy Users
- Moderate Users
- Occasional Users
- Frequent Shifters

These groups and their proportional representation in the company's customer portfolio are shown in Figure 4–4. As the figure indicates, individual Heavy Users generate an average profit of $300 per year for the company. At the other end of the customer spectrum, Frequent Shifters are costly to serve, each one creating a $50 loss over the course of a year. Occasional Users are nothing to chase after either, contributing only $50 per customer per year to the bottom line. Worse still, these last two categories account for 65 percent of all customers in the company's portfolio. The average customer value for XYZ is $92.50.

Obviously, this company would be better off if it could either eliminate the Frequent Shifters or develop them into Occasional or higher-level users. Likewise, upgrading Moderate Users to Heavy Users would increase the value of the company's franchise. And just a small change in this direction could produce impressive

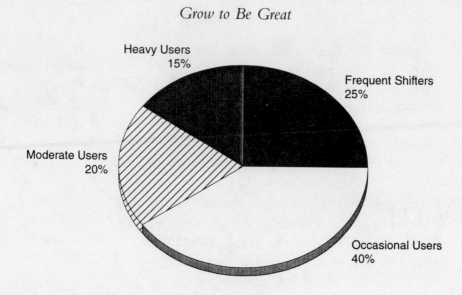

Figure 4–4. The XYZ Customer Portfolio
Source: Mercer Management Consulting analysis.

bottom-line results. Consider for a moment what would happen if XYZ company reduced each of its bottom tier categories by five percent and increased its two top tier categories in the same proportion.

Heavy Users	15% to 20%
Moderate Users	20% to 25%
Occasional Users	40% to 35%
Frequent Shifters	25% to 20%

These shifts are undramatic, but they create dramatic bottom-line change, increasing the average customer value by 27 percent, to $117.50. How many companies would like to create that much growth in a single year?

When we look at companies with high and sustained growth, we see that these shifts are achieved through careful attention to one or more of the following activities: acquisition, development, and retention of customers. Underlying these activities is a clear understanding of the value of individual customers or customer segments.

Selective customer acquisition

Choosing the right customers to focus on is the most important element in building a customer franchise. Customer acquisition begins with a detailed knowledge of current and potential customers. Who are they? What do they have in common? Which are the most attractive customers and segments—the ones that add the greatest value to our franchise?

In general, the most attractive acquisitions are those that display a high degree of preference for the seller's product or service and are profitable to serve. Those with a high profit potential but a low degree of preference may also be attractive if the product or service can be redesigned or repositioned to attract them. Among those with a high degree of preference we must watch out for customers with low profit potential; these may be easy to acquire, but will consume resources with little or no return to the company.

Just as USAA discovered that a very profitable business does not necessarily come from the most affluent customer segment, other practitioners of customer franchise management have found their target segments in underserved parts of the population. Enterprise Rent-A-Car, for example, has grown to become a larger company, by some measures, than Hertz. While Hertz competes against a large number of sophisticated, well-funded competitors for the business travel market, Enterprise has found its fortune in supplying replacement vehicles to consumers whose cars are in the repair shop.

Sometimes several companies can find high profits in the same industry by successfully focusing on very different customer segments. Southwest Airlines and British Airways, for example, are two of the most profitable airlines in the world. Each focuses on a very different customer segment in the air travel market. Southwest has perfected a low-cost, low-price, no-frills service, while British Airways targets the business traveler with amenities that include a free shower and clothes pressing upon arrival in London.

McDonald's likewise offers an example of the fine art of selective customer acquisition. On the surface, you'd think that this fast-food chain was indifferent to who walked through the door, as long as they have money in their pockets. The menu appeals to people in most demographic groups, and the prices are affordable to just about anyone.

Dig a little deeper and you'll notice that McDonald's restaurants do not have large banks of public telephones. There are no video arcades or anything else that might say to teenagers, "This is a great place to *hang out*." In McDonald's advertising the only teenagers are working behind the counter. Look around some more and you'll notice that every McDonald's has large, clean restrooms, the type that mothers with children will stop to visit. And they do visit regularly, giving rise to the observation we heard from a group of mothers that McDonald's is "America's restroom." Many of these same restaurants have mini-playgrounds for small children.

Without saying so, McDonald's has created a combination of food and surroundings that is a welcome mat for families while removing incentives for teenagers to hang out.

Figure 4–5 provides a graphic representation of the challenge of selective customer acquisition. A company's core franchise is those customers for whom the firm's product and delivery capabilities are in sync. For USAA, this core is military officers. For the *Wall Street Journal,* it's business managers and business professionals. These customers see the firm's products or services as representing greater value than competing alternatives. The firm is able to service these customers at relatively low cost, making their business highly profitable.

Figure 4–5 underscores the all too common fallacy of aiming for "market share." For most companies, the goal of capturing the dominant market share leads them into wasteful efforts to sell to customers who are either unprofitable to serve, or who have rational resistance to the company's products or service—the group in the upper left of the figure. It is almost always better to pursue "frontier customers," for whom current products are not quite right or for whom the current delivery systems are not optimal. There are essentially two ways to do this: (1) enhancing a product's value to those customers who currently prefer an alternative product (a marketing challenge), or (2) delivering the existing product more efficiently to customers who like it but are not willing to pay for it (a process design challenge).

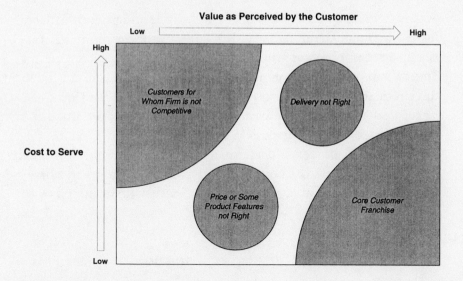

Figure 4–5. The Customer Acquisition Challenge
Source: Mercer Management Consulting analysis.

Our colleagues often point to ScrubaDub, a Boston-area car wash chain, as a company that has extended its core franchise by enhancing product value in the eyes of potential customers for whom that product was perceived as "not quite right." ScrubaDub is one of those rare companies that has operationalized what virtually all business pundits cite as the keys to success: service and quality that exceed expectations, intimate knowledge of customers, and integration of that knowledge with operations. ScrubaDub captures customer information by enrolling many of them in its "club" and by "bar coding" members' vehicles. The bar code sticker makes it possible for ScrubaDub to know its customers' names, the car models they drive, their service preferences, their frequency of use, even when to send out birthday coupons for a free wash.

One big payoff of this system relative to extending the franchise was the discovery that Mercedes and Lexus drivers were underrepresented in the company's list of customers. A little investigation explained why. Visits to local Mercedes and Lexus dealers revealed that purchasers of these high-priced automobiles were told to avoid commercial car washes because their cleaning solutions were judged by manufacturers to be damaging to these cars' highly finished surfaces. This was true for most car washes but not true for ScrubaDub, whose detergents were specially formulated to avoid this problem. ScrubaDub took the time to educate Mercedes and Lexus dealers in its service areas about the safety of its product, and even induced them to include a free ScrubaDub coupon in each new car buyer's packet of dealer materials. This not only overcame the barrier between the company and a valuable segment of drivers, but put the dealer's imprimatur on ScrubaDub as the place to get a "safe" car wash.

Customer development

Acquiring the right customers, while critical, is only the beginning of franchise management. Developing the value of the customer relationship calls for increasing the volume of purchases, the margin on those purchases, and the duration of the relationship.

In many businesses—car washes, credit cards, and air travel— firms attempt to build volume per customer by increasing "share of wallet," that is, the number of times a customer uses the firm's product or service versus those of competitors. ScrubaDub's average customer comes in for a car wash six times each year; its "club" members more than a dozen times each year.

In banking, the goal is to "cross-sell" related services such as mutual funds, financial planning, and so forth. However, as many bank customers who have tried to receive favorable treatment on a mortgage rate refinancing have discovered, most banks are so organized around products that they fail to view the customer relationship as a whole and extend no special treatment to the customer.

Efforts to increase the margin or rate of profit on customer purchase streams too often rely almost entirely on trying to extract a price premium from loyal customers. Instead of reinforcing their loyalty through price concessions, many companies try to squeeze their customers for more, and in the process drive them away. Analysis of the insurance industry indicates that the expected "firm renewal rate" drops from 50 percent to 25 percent following a 10 percent price increase.

In many cases, customer development is fostered by extensive customer databases. Fingerhut, a catalog merchandiser, maintains an extensive (1,400 data elements per household) customer database that supports 75 specialty catalogs and 150 personalized mailings each year. Zeppelin Metallwerke, the dominant distributor of Caterpillar, maintains a detailed database on more than 20,000 customers that includes equipment usage patterns and service records. This enables them to provide an exceptional parts inventory and to secure the aftermarket business.

Opportunities to develop current customers are abundant, and sometimes just being a good listener will reveal them. L.L. Bean enjoys one of the strongest customer franchises in the outdoor clothing/equipment industry, and it knows how to listen for opportunities to sell more to its current customers. Bean has developed a system for registering, coding, and analyzing the thousands of comments that its customer service operators pick up in the normal course of business every week. In one instance, these comments led to the development of a new line of L.L. Bean clothes for children. Customers were asking, "Can I get parkas and outfits like these for my kids?"

Customer retention

Extending the duration of the customer relationship is the third major customer value-building strategy. You may have heard the term "zero defections." Some companies view this as an important goal—right up there with zero defects and 100 percent customer satisfaction. Unfortunately, unless these companies have zero unprofitable customers, they are shooting themselves in *both* feet—actually spending energy and money to retain customers who create more costs than profits. We have a successful stockbroker friend who takes just the opposite approach. One of his annual goals is to "fire" a number of his clients. As he describes them, "these are the clients who are always calling to talk, to complain, to second guess our market research, or otherwise take up our time. Some are profitable to me and the firm but are so difficult to deal with as individuals that they make my work unpleasant. I'd rather spend my time and energy on other customers." One of the most profitable credit card issuers told us that they regularly write to unprofitable customers asking them to leave.

Retention is just one of the areas in which the principles of customer valuation pay off. Once you know which customers have the greatest value or potential value, retention efforts can be focused on keeping them—and only them. Let your competitors steal all the deadwood from your portfolio. With the value of individual customers or customer segments understood, we can calculate the cost of each defection and, based on this calculation, devise a cost-effective strategy for customer retention. This strategy should concentrate on profitable customers who exhibit a propensity for switching. Again, resources currently wasted on unprofitable customers can be invested in keeping these customers.

In the banking industry, the Council on Financial Competition has done studies on the value of different classes of retail customers, what each defection costs a banking institution, and how these defections can be stemmed. For bankers, individual customers represent a stream of annuity-like payments over time. The longer a customer stays with a bank, the larger his or her balances tend to grow. Demand deposit accounts, for example, tend to grow at a compound annual rate of 8 percent. Profitable cross-selling opportunities grow dramatically with the longevity of an account, but without proportional increases in servicing costs.

Based on this type of information, bank managers have been able to create strategies for retaining high-value customers. For example, many defections result when customers move to new geographic locations. Often, however, these new locations are within the service areas of branch banks. With very little cost, bank managers have found that simply introducing the departing customer to a service representative at the appropriate branch is all it takes to save the account. Balances and signature cards are transferred with no inconvenience to the customer.

THE WALGREENS GROWTH MACHINE

The examples cited so far are largely success stories in businesses where it is possible to identify the individual customer at every transaction. Airlines, banks, mail-order companies, and even car washes have the ability to assign account numbers to customers and to develop highly sophisticated information about each one. What happens when the customer is anonymous? Few companies manage this problem as well as Walgreens.

As the largest drugstore chain in the United States, Walgreens has enjoyed two decades of uninterrupted profitable growth. Currently an $8 billion company, century-old Walgreens has posted record sales and earnings in each of the past ten years, and its annual rate of growth has regularly been in the double digits. As a measure of its prowess, the stock market currently values each square foot of Walgreens' selling space at slightly more than double the average for other drugstore chains.

What sets Walgreens apart from its competitors is the way it views its business. Most retailers think about asset productivity in terms of buildings, inventories, and square footage. Walgreens focuses on the productivity of its customer assets—sales and costs per customer. Instead of appealing to the "average" customer, Walgreens determines which customers are the most productive and focuses on them. The result: its sales per square foot of floor space is 50 percent to 100 percent higher than its competitors.

Our research into a broad set of drugstore competitors in one major market area showed that Walgreens' higher sales per square foot do not result from a larger customer base. In fact, its typical store has a slightly smaller clientele than the average drugstore, and the dollar value of the average transaction at a Walgreens is lower than at its competitors. The greater sales result from the fact that Walgreens' customers visit the store *twice as often* as other chains' customers. High-frequency shoppers—those who visit a drugstore more than five times monthly— make up only 10 percent of the population but account for almost half of Walgreens' sales. Walgreens' share of these high-frequency shoppers is three times that of one of its major competitors.

By understanding a representative sample of customers, forming experimental segments and carefully tracking their responses to merchandise assortments and store amenities, it is possible for retailers to continuously refine the quality of service to a group of people whom it does not know as individuals. The use of credit cards, frequent shopper clubs or other data gathering devices has enabled some retailers to gather specific customer information. But for a high-frequency, low-price business such as drugstores, this may not be practical or cost effective.

The coherence of Walgreens' customer franchise strategy is striking. By targeting and acquiring high-value customers, it generates superior sales throughput, which in turn generates the enormous cash flow that fuels the company's investments in new markets, store renovations, and operational improvements. These investments, coupled with a near fanatical commitment to continuous improvement and a willingness to experiment, increase the stream of sales and profits. With high-value customer assets as its engine, Walgreens has built a powerful growth machine (Figure 4–6).

High-frequency drugstore customers come in all ages, genders, and incomes, defying the standard segmentations. What they have in common is a perception of the drugstore as a convenient place to buy many items normally found at supermarkets, convenience food outlets, and discount merchandise stores. Convenience is their overriding concern, and they are willing to pay a premium for it. Purchase frequency, demonstrated store loyalty, and a willingness to trade price for convenience make these customers highly profitable to acquire, develop, and retain.

Make it easy for target customers to do business with you

Determining which customers to acquire is only the start. The next step is to figure out *how* to capture them. For retailers, whose doors are open to all, this is a real challenge. USAA doesn't face this problem; its market is defined by its charter, and the fact that it deals mostly through direct marketing channels gives it tremendous con-

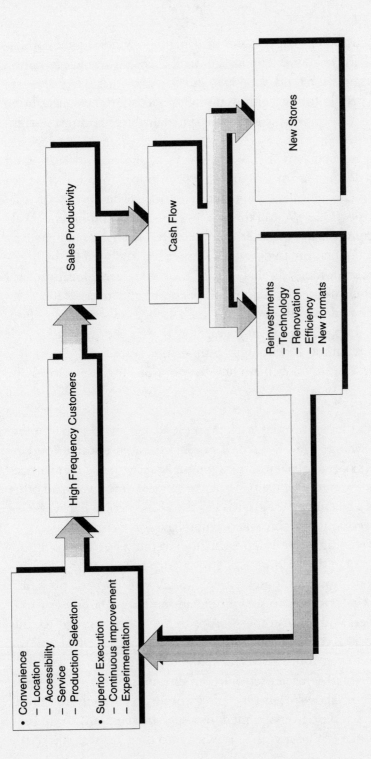

Figure 4–6. The Walgreens Growth Machine
Source: Mercer Management Consulting analysis.

trol over customer selection and management. Mutual fund companies and banks likewise discourage small accounts by simply raising the minimums for fund purchases and bank services. They encourage busy people to stay with them by providing exceptional phone services. But how does a drugstore on Main Street bring the right customers through the door?

What's needed here is the systematic application of marketing tools and levers—from pricing and promotion to product selection—to facilitate the selection and retention of the most profitable customer portfolio. We call this process "customer fulfillment." Walgreens' approach to customer fulfillment has been, through analysis and experimentation, to develop a store format tailored to the high-frequency customer. All characteristics of the store—location, layout, product selection, pricing, and operating practices—reflect the company's understanding of *where* high-frequency customers shop, *how* they shop, and *what* they shop for. It uses the most advanced checkout scanning technology to make the customer's experience quicker and more convenient and to monitor purchase patterns.

What can other companies learn from the Walgreens example? A few important things. One is that it is possible through research to identify clusters of potential customers whose *behaviors* make them attractive. In the case of Walgreens, demographics, income levels, and other traditional groupings mean much less than how people behave—that is, their need to make convenience purchases on a regular basis.

To serve a single customer segment extremely well can, as it does at USAA, form the basis of very strong corporate strategy. Any single segment, however, poses limits. USAA will be hard pressed if the military continues to shrink. Expansion to the families of military officers and to customer groups that might be similar to military officers is underway. Serving multiple groups well can be the basis for an even more powerful strategy. This strategy is less difficult, however, if you can separate the channels of communication to them. This allows each type of customer to see only the product features and pricing designed for a specific segment. Sometimes the difference can be invisible, as when two travelers walk up to the same airline ticket counter and pay the same price for the same flight, but one is quietly upgraded to first class because the reservations computer alerts the counter clerk to the traveler's status as a frequent flyer. But there are businesses in which the same value proposition must be offered to all comers. In this case, it may not be possible to serve every desired segment differentially. Instead, the value proposition needs to be designed to attract the best possible mix of segments—to be the *first* choice for high-value customers and a *good* choice for others.

One such business is gasoline retailing. Having invested in real estate on which to operate a network of gas stations, the retail marketer is faced with a bewildering variety of choices in designing a service offering. Pricing, self service or full service, repairs, parts, car washes, convenience stores, fast-food restaurants, diesel fuel, automatic teller machines, hours of operation, and other factors can all be considered in the design of each site. Each decision adds to or subtracts from the cost of building and operating sites. Each decision makes the entire network more or less attractive in the eyes of a particular type of customer.

Unlike USAA's military officer customers, gasoline buyers wear no uniform to identify the segment to which they belong. Each buyer, however, has an integrated set of needs and attitudes about buying gasoline that leads them to choose one offering over another. By careful analysis it is possible to identify segments of customers with similar "clusters" of those needs. Through customer franchise methodology it also is possible to quantify the value of each segment based on its size, its potential revenues (from purchases of fuels by octane type and other "ancillary services" such as convenience stores, car washes and so forth) and cost to serve. Figure 4–7 shows a typical list of retail petroleum customer segments.

The retailer faces several challenges. First, the combination of offerings must be "pure" enough to attract certain segments. For example, credit card activated self service pumps and convenience stores both attract the "speedy shopper" segment—but friendly, collegial service (which is valued by the "neighborhood mechanic user segment") could take too long and turn the "speedy shoppers" off. The offerings have to be aligned to appeal to the full set of customer needs.

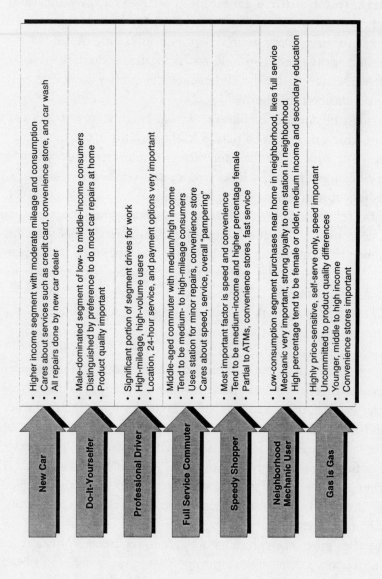

New Car
- Higher income segment with moderate mileage and consumption
- Cares about services such as credit card, convenience store, and car wash
- All repairs done by new car dealer

Do-It-Yourselfer
- Male-dominated segment of low- to middle-income consumers
- Distinguished by preference to do most car repairs at home
- Product quality important

Professional Driver
- Significant portion of segment drives for work
- High-mileage, high-volume users
- Location, 24-hour service, and payment options very important

Full Service Commuter
- Middle-aged commuter with medium/high income
- Tend to be medium- to high-mileage consumers
- Uses station for minor repairs, convenience store
- Cares about speed, service, overall "pampering"

Speedy Shopper
- Most important factor is speed and convenience
- Tend to be medium-income and higher percentage female
- Partial to ATMs, convenience stores, fast service

Neighborhood Mechanic User
- Low-consumption segment purchases near home in neighborhood, likes full service
- Mechanic very important, strong loyalty to one station in neighborhood
- High percentage tend to be female or older, medium income and secondary education

Gas is Gas
- Highly price-sensitive, self-serve only, speed important
- Uncommitted to product quality differences
- Younger, middle to high income
- Convenience stores important

Figure 4–7. Retail Gasoline Customer Segments
Source: Mercer Management Consulting analysis.

Conversely, the offering should be designed, if possible, to appeal positively to more than just the core segment. For example, the needs of the "speedy shopper" segment are not *too* different from those of the "new car" segment (if additional services are added) or the "gas is gas" segment (if price is competitive).

Third, all of this takes place in a competitive context—the offering not only has to map up well against the integrated needs of the target segment, but it must be executed in a manner *superior to competition*. A service-based positioning requires the best service in the business to succeed. In retailing, like in poker, being second best can be an extremely expensive proposition.

One of the best practitioners we know of this demanding art is Caltex. A joint venture of Texaco and Chevron, Caltex does all its business overseas, though it is headquartered in the United States. With over 15,000 retail sites in 60 Asian and African countries, Caltex sells $14 billion of petroleum products every year to a wide variety of customer types.

In 1992–93, Chairman and CEO Pat Ward instituted a program of customer franchise management across all of Caltex's markets in response to competitive actions that threatened to erode the company's market share. For every country, the cluster analysis pointed to a specific mix of features that needed to be included for Caltex to be most competitive with the features competitors were offering to the most attractive segments in that country.

Caltex undertook a massive program to reposition its stations in its eight largest markets. Not only was the research complex, but the implementation required that every major business process be reexamined to provide the best support to the new strategy in each country and benchmarked against the best competitors in the world. Figure 4–8 lists the major processes that needed to be changed in each country in order for Caltex to actually deliver on the unique value proposition that was planned. By early 1995, Caltex was gaining market share in every major market where it had implemented the plan.

Chairman Ward captured the importance of not only designing a superior offering to specific customers but also undertaking the

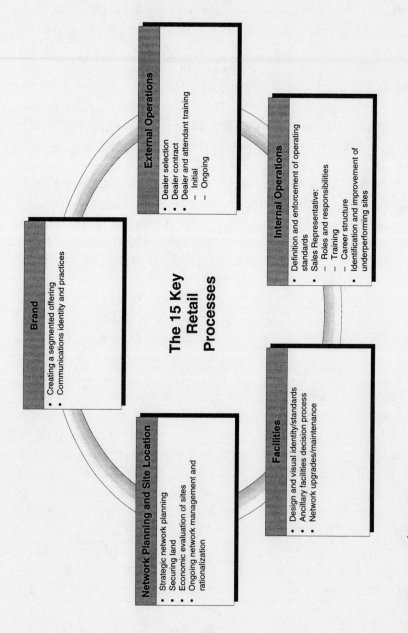

Figure 4–8. Key Retail Processes

Source: Mercer Management Consulting analysis.

full range of activities necessary to deliver that offering profitably when he wrote to Caltex management: "The overall objective of Caltex is to become the brand of choice in targeted retail segments. This statement is both a brand position communicated to our customers and a way of doing business which places demands on the entire organization."

THE ENABLERS OF CUSTOMER FRANCHISE MANAGEMENT

USAA, Walgreens, Caltex, and other practitioners of Customer Franchise Management have learned to find specific customer segments within the broad mass of the marketplace, to determine the needs of those segments, to find ways to profitably serve those needs, and to create levels of satisfaction and loyalty that translate into business growth.

We are convinced that for every group of potential customers very well served by a company like USAA, many more such groups lie unidentified and underserved. *Find them, serve them, and become a growth leader.*

5

NEW PRODUCT AND SERVICE DEVELOPMENT

✳

At first glance, the introduction of new products would seem to be one of the oldest growth strategies on the planet. Business history and business mythology are often told in terms of a series of great inventions. Indeed, some versions of American history tell the story of the nation as a string of new products stretching from interchangeable parts and the cotton gin through the automobile and the airplane to the television and the computer.

It has always been possible to build a successful company around a great new idea. But this is not the phenomenon we are describing when we refer to a *strategy* of new product development. The occasional discovery of a stunning new technology will continue to create new legends to stand alongside Eli Whitney and Thomas Edison. If your company has such an invention, enjoy it. Most of these inventions, however, tend to occur only once in the life of a given company and stem from some combination of genius and luck.

More interesting to us, from a management point of view, are the companies that deliver steady streams of successful new products and services in the absence of the "Eureka Solution." For these companies, sustained growth is more attributable to strategy than to inspiration and inventive genius. There is a pattern in the behavior of companies with histories of successful new product introductions. We believe that this pattern offers useful lessons to managers, that it represents a significant change from the way in which most general managers have learned to think about new products, and that companies seeking to improve their records in this area are not addressing the issues that prevent them from succeeding.

THE EVOLUTION OF
NEW PRODUCT DEVELOPMENT

Managers often bemoan the fact that the art of management has produced so little that is *really* new. New product development, however, is one domain of management in which this complaint cannot be justified. Today's senior executives have seen major improvements, each building upon its predecessors.

In the 1960s, new product developers brought new, sophisticated techniques to the demands of highly complex *project management*. The Polaris missile and submarine project was probably the most technologically sophisticated and complex development project that mankind had tackled up to that point in time. Nevertheless, it was managed with such skill that nearly every piece of the complex puzzle fell into place exactly when it was supposed to. Polaris is often cited as the source of new insights about the interrelatedness of multiple activities in a complex project.

The PERT (Program Evaluation Review Technique) chart, developed during the Polaris project, and related tools developed during the 1960s brought new precision to the management of large, messy projects and to the introduction of complicated new products and services.

But few new product projects have enjoyed the success of the Polaris program. A tremendous number ended as failures—many as expensive failures. The increasing cost of failure shifted the focus of product developers in the 1970s to the issue of *risk reduction*. To reduce the risk of failure, leading companies built elaborate testing and periodic reviews into their project plans. "Stage gates" assessed progress at each step of the development process, determining whether projects should continue and whether they were being well managed.

Although new product projects were rationally managed and

constantly checked for potential threats to ultimate success, review committees and progress assessments began to take a toll in time and money, especially for complex projects.

In seeking to minimize risk, new product developers discovered a new risk: the risk that somebody else might get to the marketplace first. In the 1980s this risk grew larger as a number of very successful companies adopted *time to market* as a competitive weapon. By restructuring the project management process and using tools like concurrent engineering, product developers made dramatic reductions in the time between idea and new product launch.

The new product development masters of the 1990s take advantage of all the lessons of the past 30 years. The best of them have raised the competitive crossbar still farther—they excel at the rapid and continuous introduction of whole families of successful new products and services. It is the *strategy of moving the entire pipeline faster* that characterizes the new product development winners today. Components of this strategy are specific and open to emulation. Some of them build upon the lessons of the past, while others are new. Optimally combined and practiced, they form one of the most viable strategies for growth.

HOW GOOD ARE TODAY'S BEST NEW PRODUCT DEVELOPERS?

The value of a strategy built around new product and service development can be seen in several ways. One is the extent to which a growing revenue base relies on new products and services. Table 5–1 shows the extent to which some prominent companies rely on new products.

What is most striking in this table is the fact that these are not new companies. Hewlett-Packard leads the list but is among the older firms in its industry. So these records do not stem from revolutionary (and/or lucky) single innovations. They stem from the *management* of innovation. Each company has, for example, stated a specific goal for the role new products will play in its growth.

TABLE 5–1

Percentage of Revenue Derived from Products and
Services Introduced in the Last Five Years

Company	Percent of Revenue
Hewlett-Packard	60%
Gillette	35%
Rubbermaid	33%
3M	30%
Corning	25%
Johnson & Johnson	25%

Source: Product Development and Management Association.

The correlation between new product development and successful growth is not limited to anecdotal examples. A 1991 survey by the Product Development and Management Association found, within specific industries, a strong correlation between competitive success and the generation of high levels of revenue from new products (Figure 5–1).

WHEN IT'S DONE RIGHT: PRODUCT DEVELOPMENT AT HEWLETT-PACKARD

It is hard to find *any* company of *any* size in *any* industry that demonstrates the power of new product strategy more impressively than Hewlett-Packard. When it comes to developing high-tech products in the fields of computers, printers, plain-paper fax machines, plotters, high-end calculators, and scientific measurement devices, this corporate giant moves with a speed and agility that few companies can match. And despite its age and size, it never seems to quit innovating and replacing its successful products with new ones that are better and cheaper. As Chairman/CEO Lew Platt has said, "We have to be willing to cannibalize what we're

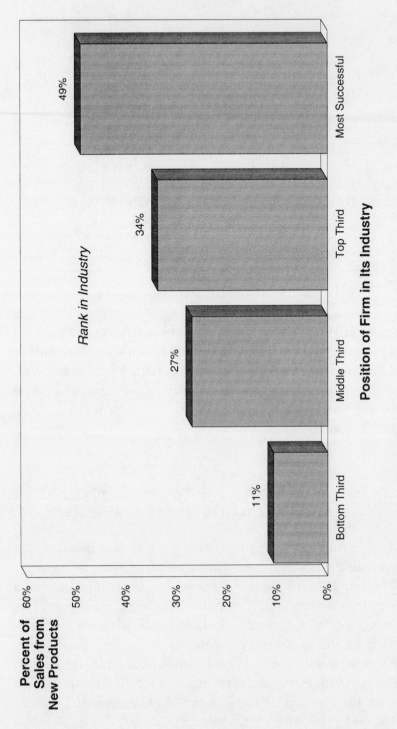

Figure 5–1. Successful Companies Generate More Revenue from New Products

Source: 1991 Product Development and Management Association Survey of 200 companies.

doing today in order to ensure our leadership in the future. . . . You have to be willing to kill your business while it is still working."[1]

We needn't look further than Hewlett-Packard's computer printer division to appreciate the company's strategy for introducing a continuous stream of new products that offer great value to customers—usually at the expense of its current products. Instead of resting on its dominance in laser printers—the high end of the market, where machines typically cost over $1,000—Hewlett-Packard developed ink-jet technology for individuals and small businesses. Today, its DeskWriter printers deliver near-laser quality printing for as little as $300. And the reliability of these machines is truly amazing. Many models and successive product generations have spun off this technology, producing tremendous growth for the company. With more than $7 billion in revenues, Hewlett-Packard's computer printer division alone could rank as a Fortune 500 company!

Nor is Hewlett-Packard shy about expanding into highly contested markets. Within the last six years it has invaded the lucrative workstation market, capturing significant share from the masters of that product segment: Sun Microsystems, IBM, and Digital Equipment. More recently, it has emerged from nowhere to become the ninth-largest worldwide shipper of personal computers.[2]

WHEN IT'S NOT DONE RIGHT: THE SAD CASE OF PROJECT COMPASS

For some readers, the example of Hewlett-Packard may bring complete clarity to the issue of new product development. For others, however, a case study of failure may be more instructive.

One of our colleagues was asked to study the management practices of a large, high-technology company that clearly was not succeeding in new product development. Management wanted to know what it was doing wrong.

He began by examining the history of one of the company's failed new product introductions—Project Compass. In doing so, he developed not only an explanation for the failure of this single product, but an explanation of why this company's attempt to compete had been so frustrating.

Project Compass was an ambitious new product program involving dozens of talented people and a five-year, multimillion dollar budget. When our colleague became involved, Compass had one highly visible problem: the product had been launched but nobody was buying. In the course of a detailed (and painful) examination of the project, several other, less visible problems came to light:

- The product addressed some customer needs that no longer existed. And those needs that still did exist were met by a competitor's product that was widely installed throughout the customer base.
- At current manufacturing costs, Compass could never make a profit—even assuming the existence of customers!
- Field sales and support personnel were actively *discouraging* the sale of Compass because their commissions were higher on other company products.

In short, Compass failed all three of our tests for a growth strategy, or a growth product. It offered inferior *value,* its *economics* were not attractive, and the organization was not *aligned to execute.* This was truly the "new product from hell." The question was, how did a company full of smart people manage to create it?

Reconstructing the history of the Compass project brought to light key points about how the company managed its pipeline of new product projects. Instead of managing the Compass project in terms of timeliness in the market, the company had focused solely on whether its internal process could produce it. Result: Compass was late to market. In fact, it had missed the market.

Second, the company never came to terms with the problems associated with the project; it simply allowed them to drift. Compass was known in the company as a troubled project for years before its launch. Its budget was a matter of annual controversy. Every stage review had approved Compass's moving on to the next stage in spite of widespread concerns. At lower levels, it became known as "the project that would not die."

Third, the Compass team had constantly battled for resources. Every assignment of personnel to Compass and every new engineering expenditure had resulted in intense infighting. Fourth, some of the most expensive and risky parts of Compass duplicated efforts being made elsewhere in the corporation. Fifth, the company failed to learn from its mistakes. Just about every mistake made during development of Compass had been made many times before in the company.

Slow development, the failure to kill bad projects, battling over resources, redundant and overlapping development efforts, and a propensity to make the same mistakes over and over again are the symptoms of a poorly managed corporate new product development strategy. What, then, are the cures for these symptoms? What are the components of a successful strategy?

THE ELEMENTS OF DOING IT RIGHT

The product development performance of Hewlett-Packard and the company that sponsored Project Compass are quite obviously many miles apart. Research jointly conducted by our firm and *R&D Magazine* in 1994 indicates that this type of performance gap takes a number of forms. In comparing companies that lead their industries in overall business performance and those that trail, we noted that higher performers:

- Experience greater financial success with the products they launch
- Actually launch a greater percentage of projects that reach advanced development stages (61 percent versus 46 percent)
- Are twice as likely to complete projects on schedule
- Are three times as likely to complete projects on budget

We believe this kind of performance has three important requirements. The first is a good system for managing individual projects. We call this "project execution." Many of the advances of the last 30 years have been in this area. Some, in particular those skills required to be first to market, do not seem to be fully adapted.

The second requirement is a supportive infrastructure for the management of multiple projects. Here as well, many companies have developed training for development personnel, customer research capabilities, physical facilities for development work, and other investments to ensure that multiple projects will succeed.

It might be argued that these first two requirements have become the "table stakes" for a business strategy that emphasizes new products—necessary but not sufficient to win. To win, companies need to master a third requirement: a set of skills for *managing the entire pipeline* of new product development efforts. This is the capability that seems to distinguish the most successful product introducers today.

Let's consider each of the three success requirements for product development.

PROJECT EXECUTION

Although the management of individual development projects is where the most work has been done for the longest time, many companies still lack mastery in this area. At the same time, the real leaders continue to generate new ideas for project management. In particular, companies seeking to keep up with the best in this area should pay attention to management of the "funnel" and to customer involvement, time to market, and the use of development teams.

Management of the funnel

Competitive winners in the new product field know how to manage a specific project. They write realistic project plans that recognize at the outset which types of resources will be required and how they must interrelate in order for the project to succeed. They use commonly agreed to, customer-centered, disciplined approaches to development projects.

Successful product developers are also careful to kill a suitable percentage of their projects early enough in the pipeline that sufficient resources are conserved for the expensive development and rollout of potential winners. Less successful companies have so many projects reaching the advanced phases of development that none can be fully funded. The rate at which the funnel narrows should be carefully considered so that the most successful new products are launched with the available funds. One sign of poor project management is large numbers of projects either killed late in the process or idled for lack of funding.

Customer involvement

More successful product innovators involve customers at all stages of the process. This involvement is particularly helpful early in the process when products are defined, target customers identified, and the basic value proposition laid out. Nearly every company somehow involves the customer late in the process, whether through test marketing or the use of beta sites. The best do so in the beginning as well.

Development is a team sport

Although the myth of the lone inventor still appeals to all of us, cross-functional teams are more likely to win. At 3M, the team approach to development was a major factor in its 50 percent reduction in development time. The problem-solving interdependencies among manufacturing, marketing, sales, service, design, engineering, and other functions are nowhere more profound than in new product development. A new corollary to Murphy's Law is that the function absent at the development table will be the one to see the fatal flaw in the plan.

Gordon Binder, chairman and CEO of Amgen, tells the tale of the shipping department employee who recognized a "show stopper" in the company's plan to market a new drug. The bioscientists and business people who had worked on the development project failed to see what this individual understood clearly—that the new drug under development would spoil in the warehouse unless Amgen made major changes in its shipping practices. This discovery—an outcome of Amgen's team-based approach to development—averted a costly disaster.

The tasks carried out by these teams have also been streamlined through the application of reengineering methodologies. As a result of reengineering, AT&T's Consumer Communications Services business unit has tripled the number of new products it launches each year, cut time to market in half, and won the Baldrige Award.

Time to market

As early as 1983, research on high-tech firms by Donald Reinertsen pointed to a clear association between speedy product development and greater commercial success. Other researchers also found that time–based competitors needed much less operating cash and could grow some 80 percent faster than their slower rivals.[3]

Former Hewlett-Packard CEO John Young was among the first of American corporate leaders to understand and act on this important time–performance relationship. He was frustrated with the time it was taking his company to introduce new products in competition with Japanese firms. In 1986, Young issued one of his famous "stretch" goals, challenging Hewlett-Packard employees to reduce time to market by 50 percent. This challenge, and an exhaustive process of internal benchmarking, helped Hewlett-Packard become a time-to-market leader and a new product powerhouse.[4]

Today, research verifies the extent to which high-performance companies are also faster in getting products to market. Figure 5–2 shows the results of our study of high and low performers. The faster-growing companies set faster time-to-market goals and they achieve them.

SUPPORTIVE INFRASTRUCTURE:
MAKING SUCCESS POSSIBLE

Modern R&D laboratories. First-rate market research. Cross-functional development teams. Skillful use of project management tools. Human talent. These are essential for any company that

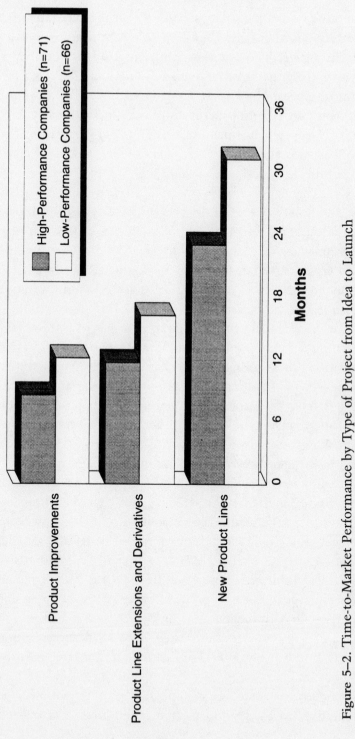

Figure 5–2. Time-to-Market Performance by Type of Project from Idea to Launch

Source: Mercer Management Consulting and *R&D Magazine* Survey, Nov. 1994.

intends to pursue a strategy based upon the development of new products. By themselves, however, they are insufficient for success. Another ingredient is required if new product development is to be a strategic driver of the business. That ingredient is a supportive infrastructure.

A supportive infrastructure is one in which resources, compensation plans, management priorities, and organizational structure are aligned with the objective of producing a continuing stream of successful new products.

One characteristic of supportive infrastructure is a high degree of attention to new products. Our research in association with *R&D Magazine* revealed that management time spent on innovation and product development was 80 percent higher among industry leaders than among their less successful competitors. Management supports also include the selection and care and feeding of project "champions."

We could hardly offer a better example of a supportive infrastructure for new product development than that of Amgen, a biopharmaceutical company whose skyrocketing growth has been propelled by its product development program. Its blood-cell growth factors—Epogen and Neupogen—enjoyed immediate success, and that success has grown with an expanding market. Company sales rose from $148 million in 1989 to $1.3 billion in 1993, making Amgen the largest U.S. biotechnology company and the thirteenth-largest pharmaceutical company in the country. Its growth rate in 1993—26 percent—was the second highest of the 16 largest pharmaceuticals companies, and its 1993 profitability (28 percent) was the highest in the entire pharmaceutical industry.

In March 1995, the *Wall Street Journal* reported that Amgen, already arguably the most successful U.S. biotech firm, had a burgeoning pipeline of new products with 11 highly promising development projects under way. Cynthia Robbins-Roth, editor of *Bio-Venture View,* reported that "Amgen has been doing a good job of quietly and capably spreading [its] tentacles around all sorts of new technology."[5]

Amgen has successfully pursued growth through a highly focused effort to develop particular products. And that effort has guided the company in its organizational structure and compensation practices, and in how management allocates its time and other resources.

From the outset, Amgen decided *not* to explore medical products on a broad scale but to concentrate on four categories of ailments, all of which share two characteristics: they cause intense suffering and they can potentially be cured or treated with drugs developed through biotechnology. If a medical product doesn't target a disease within one of the four areas, Amgen avoids it. Founder and chairman Gordon Binder said he resisted the urge to try to develop medical products that might be used in fighting other ailments. "We are only one company," he says. "We'll only do what we *can* do."

Toward that end, Binder organized Amgen in a distinctive way. Recognizing that the basic level of the biotechnology business is the molecule, every new Amgen product starts at the molecular level. If an Amgen lab researcher isolates a molecule and convinces management that it has a possibility of being turned into a drug that will treat a disease within one of the targeted categories, that molecule then becomes a business unit and the focus of a team effort headed by a "heavy-weight" project leader. Teams are the organizing principle of the company. Functional departments such as R&D, marketing, and manufacturing exist to provide teams with qualified people; they are not "steps" in the development process.

At most biotech firms, a development project would be executed through a series of "handoffs." Starting with the lab people, the project would be passed on to the people who manufacture prototype batches, to the people who do the animal testing, to the people who do the human testing, to the people who go to the FDA and run clinical trials, to the people who manufacture and package the drug, and eventually to the people who sell it to doctors. Amgen's new product development process is very different. Its single process manager has responsibility for all stages of product development and ultimate launch. That person doesn't just manage the process; he or she serves as the product's champion, responsible for convincing employees throughout the company that they should be committing themselves and their department's resources to the molecule. Since almost all employees own stock in the company, all have a vested interest in working together to create successful new products.

In many ways, form follows function at Amgen. The company has oriented itself to the requirements of developing successful bio-pharmaceutical products. Organizational structure, compensation, resource allocation, and the company's culture support a strategy of growth through new products. And it works.

As a fairly new company with a singular focus, Amgen may have an easier time with this process of organizational adaptation than would a larger company with multiple divisions. Nevertheless, it provides a useful model of the relationship between new product strategy and supportive infrastructure.

THE MOST IMPORTANT PART: MANAGING THE ENTIRE PIPELINE

The refinement of project management skills and the creation of a supportive infrastructure are, as we have said, necessary but not sufficient for a company that seeks to regularly grow through product development. The critical component of this strategy—and the piece that is so often missing—is the ability to manage the entire pipeline of new product projects and the portfolio of opportunities it represents. Portfolio management is the "hidden process" for development success. It is the least understood area in new product development and the greatest impediment to successful strategy. It is also the area in which senior managers can have the greatest impact.

Figure 5–3 is a graphic representation of the challenge to senior managers. The improved methodologies cited earlier help companies in handling individual projects. What is needed is a process for managing across projects on behalf of corporate strategy.

Before we spell out what needs to be done in this area, let's con-

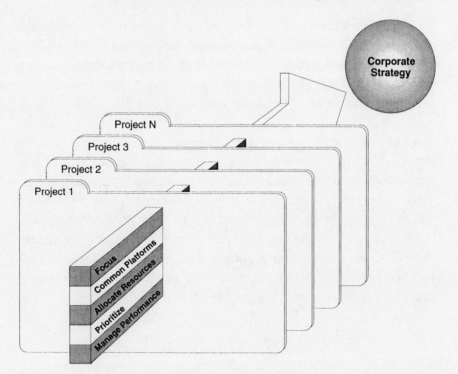

Figure 5–3. The Portfolio Management Challenge
Source: Mercer Management Consulting analysis.

sider the symptoms of malaise common in companies that *lack* a meaningful process for managing the new product portfolio:

- *Projects that never reach completion but never die.* These are the government agencies of corporate America. Once upon a time each seemed like a good idea. Today, their purposes are unclear, but they have constituencies that lobby for their continued existence and funding.
- *Conflict over resources.* When individual projects follow their own course, each feels equally entitled to scarce resources. Moreover, since what one project gets must come off the plate of another, there's plenty of conflict and lobbying.
- *Redundant development efforts.* Lack of portfolio coordination results in costly duplication of effort among projects. Both costs and time

to market increase when individual projects fail to adopt common standards, common parts, and common technologies.

- *Little or no learning from project to project.* Lacking management across projects, the company finds few opportunities to gain from experience. Lessons learned from one project are not shared with others.

These are symptoms of a lack of control and coordination at the top. To avoid them, senior management must adopt an agenda that harnesses new product development efforts as a strategic resource. This places great demands on senior managers, but gives them added leverage in ensuring the success of their product strategies.

Management of the pipeline entails five key tasks: focusing the "fuzzy" front end, selecting common platforms and technologies, managing priorities, allocating resources across projects, and managing process performance in the aggregate. Here is what we mean by each.

Focusing the "fuzzy" front end

Too often, senior managers only get seriously involved in projects at some midpoint in the development process, perhaps when a certain spending threshold is about to be passed. At this point, customer needs may already have been assessed. The questions that lurk in managers' heads now are often the same: Why are we working on this? How will it impact our other products? Why this and not something else?

These are valid questions but they have been asked too late. There is a fuzzy front end to development projects, when concepts are first formulated and the decision is made, at least implicitly, to choose some opportunities over others. Most senior managers are uninvolved at this point. They should be involved.

Questions that should be asked in the fuzzy phase include:

- Are we identifying opportunities that support the strategic direction of the company? If an idea doesn't support company strategy, are we prepared to steer the company in a new direction to support this single product?

- Has management played a role in determining which ideas enter the development pipeline and which do not?
- What are we *not* doing because we are doing this?
- What effect on our investment in new products would this project have if it went forward? Do we have the appropriate mix of entirely new ideas and enhancements to existing product lines?
- Will this project help us plan for future generations of products and the use of new technologies?

Although some companies simply play roulette with the ideas that come along, we believe that an approach built on focus is the better route.

Selecting common platforms and technologies

One of the more remarkable manufacturing developments of the past decade has been "mass customization," the production of a great variety of products—almost made to order—at mass production prices. At the heart of most mass customization efforts is the use of common "platforms" to which customizing options can be added in the final stages of production. The seemingly endless variety of Casio digital watches, for example, rests on a very small set of common platforms.

A platform is not a product but the core of components or technologies underlying a product. Often, it is the lowest-level technology common to a set of products. For example, the PowerPC microprocessor and the Macintosh operating system form the platform underlying an entire family of Apple products with many different features.

The benefits of using common platforms are many and undeniable: lower risk that the thing just won't work; faster time to market; lower manufacturing and service costs; and the opportunity to tailor products to market segments with few added costs. In addition, customers' acceptance of new products can sometimes be enhanced if they recognize a familiar and reliable platform as a key component of a new offering.

Figure 5–4 shows the effect on cycle time and unit costs when a large home electronics company switched to the use of common platforms. Almost every stage of product development took less time (and, although the chart can't depict this, was less risky). In addition, new products were produced at much lower costs early in their life cycles, when volumes were low. Because platforms cut across projects, these benefits can be obtained only when development projects are managed as a portfolio.

Common platforms provide upstream benefits as well. The number of parts that any company must order and inventory can explode if management fails to set development policies that include a list of acceptable components from which a new product may be designed. One leading electronics company had over 15,000 different types of parts in its inventory before adopting common platforms. A rigorous program of exploiting common platforms reduced the parts inventory to 1,100 types, with no perceptible effect on internal creativity or customer satisfaction. The cost savings from this parts reduction were enormous.

With entire families of products riding on common platforms, the choice of platforms becomes critical. The one benefit of not having common platforms is that a bad concept can't infiltrate an entire product line. Top management must therefore be cognizant of choices that, on a product-by-product basis, may seem like minor engineering issues but because they have an effect on platform strategy, become strategic in their impact.

A commitment to common platforms also increases the importance of the decision to *stop* using a platform. Management must constantly weigh the benefits of continued use against the risk that a platform is changing from a strength to a weakness.

Managing priorities

Even companies that are highly focused on specific customer groups or types of products have insufficient resources for developing every idea quickly and completely. As a result, competition for resources is inevitable. Success in this competition cannot hinge on who has the most friends at the top, who writes the best pro-

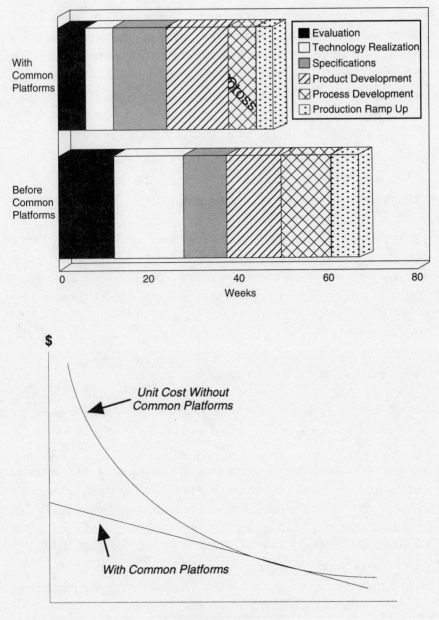

Figure 5–4. The Effect of Common Platform Use on Time to Market and Unit Cost

Source: Mercer Management Consulting analysis.

posals, or who has the most money hidden away in slush funds. Senior management has to evaluate new product projects on a cross-company basis. Those with the greatest potential for the company must be selected and given the higher priority.

Allocating resources across projects

Selecting and prioritizing development projects requires judgment and vision. These qualities must, however, be complemented by analysis that considers the firm's capacity to carry these projects forward to timely completion.

Manufacturing companies employ master schedulers to balance customer orders with the plant's capacity to produce and deliver. These schedulers understand the factory's capacity, the availability of human and material resources, and the probable location of bottlenecks given the orders on hand. Their goal is to schedule production in ways that prevent work from piling up at critical workstations, that meet customer delivery requirements, and that "load-level" work within the factory.

New product projects create analogous master scheduling problems. Consider Figure 5–5, which indicates the total requirements for a single resource, say, computer-aided design (CAD) work for Projects A, B, C, and D over a six-quarter time frame. Management has the responsibility for determining and planning CAD capacity. In the figure, demand exceeds the firm's CAD-hour capacity of 300 in several quarters, and a surplus exists in others. Management must either coordinate a shift in the timing of CAD requirements or increase capacity. Failure to do so will obviously result in delays for certain projects, as CAD capacity creates bottlenecks.

The failure to manage resources, as in this simple example, typically results in the following problems:

- Queues form as critical shared functions become overloaded
- Project planning takes place without knowledge of firmwide resources or capacities
- Personnel are stretched over too many projects

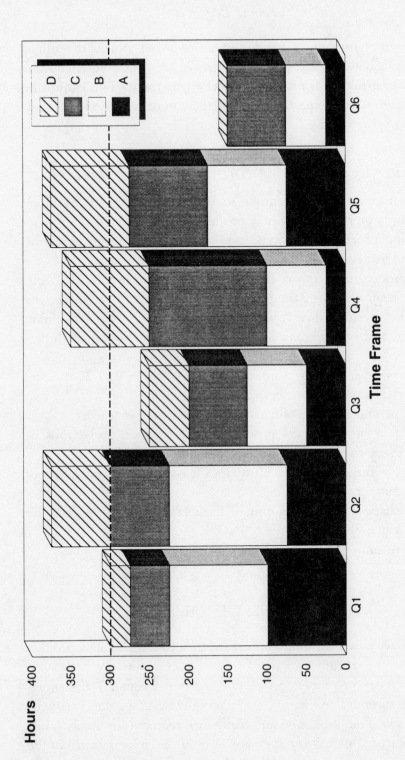

Figure 5–5. CAD Capacity Planning
Source: Mercer Management Consulting analysis.

These problems can be avoided by an ongoing process that aligns projects and available resources, that anticipates and resolves bottlenecks, and that plans future resource requirements. This cannot be done from within a particular project; it can only be done through portfolio management.

Managing process performance in the aggregate

As we implied in the foregoing scheduling example, the development of large numbers of new products can be viewed as a manufacturing process of its own. Just as careful measurement of the right variables can improve the flow of the production line, the same process can improve the development flow of new products. Those responsible for the process as a whole need to choose the set of key performance variables, create practical metrics for them, and watch them carefully. Some of these variables might include:

- The number of new products introduced each year. How does this compare with our competitors?
- The percentage of products that become market leaders.
- The percentage of new products that meet their projections, or earn back the cost of their development.
- Average time to market. How does it compare with the best of our competitors?
- The shape of our development funnel. How many projects are killed at each stage?
- The revenue percentage derived from new products.

THE ROLE OF THE CEO

We believe that managing a steady stream of successful new product introductions requires a careful mix of bottom-up and top-down influence on the process. As we will argue in Chapter 7, the *organizational alignment* necessary for new product development is particularly tricky. The inspiration and hard work required for a new product to succeed may come from any level of the organization, but the leadership to introduce common platforms and to manage the port-folio of projects often must come from the CEO. One friend of ours likens this arrangement to that of an orchestra: a group of highly skilled individuals who could be very competent soloists play accord-ing to the tempo and interpretation imposed by the conductor.

One conductor whose orchestra has played very well lately is Alfred Zeien, CEO of Gillette. A decade ago, this famous company almost fell victim to a hostile takeover. Corporate raiders charged that the company had become tired, and that its globally known brand name was not being used as an asset for growth. Gillette maintained its inde-pendence and, shortly thereafter, Zeien assumed the chief executive's role. Since that time, Gillette's edge has become razor sharp.

New product introductions are clearly creating growth for the company. Since 1990, for example, its Sensor razor has led the company to 54 percent growth in the United States and 71 per-cent worldwide in razor and blade sales, in spite of the fact that the Sensor was, to some extent, cannibalizing sales of existing Gillette shaving products.

We caught up with Zeien on one of the rare occasions when he was spending the entire day in his office overlooking Boston's Back Bay district. He confirmed that Gillette observes nearly all of the practices that we have identified with superior new product devel-opment. And the results are clear. In the 1980s, the company was introducing eight to ten new products each year. Now, the pace has more than doubled, with more than 20 new product introductions annually—almost two a month. In addition, management has worked to reduce the time required for "rollout," the process by which a new product is introduced into all of Gillette's markets. For a company that gathers 70 percent of its revenues outside the United States, this is a critical part of the development launch process. The highly successful Sensor razor took four years to expand from its first market area to full global coverage. Gillette today aims to manage the process in half the time.

The funnel for new products at Gillette is carefully managed to generate a high number of development projects. On average, each product actually launched is the survivor of three products that were developed in prototype. These three products were, in turn, culled from 15 development projects. In order to continue its pace of more than 20 new product introductions each year, Gillette must begin over 300 development projects annually, almost one a day. If 300 projects are to be managed intelligently to yield 20 products, the process of killing most of them and nurturing the survivors must be very carefully managed.

A variety of inputs is used to evaluate projects. Consumer research identifies attractive and unattractive features of potential new products. Manufacturing costs and feasibility are considered very early. Indeed, the most common reason for discontinuing a Gillette project is manufacturing cost.

Cross-functional teams are used to ensure maximum breadth of input. Project champions are identified early and encouraged to provide aggressive leadership to the project, although, as Zeien was careful to point out, "if the idea just isn't feasible after we have done our best thinking, the champion must know that he is not going to be shot." This helps to prevent projects from hanging on grimly while those involved worry more about their careers than about whether the proposed product will actually help the company.

What does Alfred Zeien do as CEO to tap the potential of this impressive growth machine? He emphasizes the importance of heavy senior management involvement early in the process. He and his senior executives are in the field each month, visiting Gillette's four basic research labs and seven development facilities. With this direct and regular contact, they develop a feel "in the stomach" for the potential of each new product idea. By his own reckoning, 30 to 35 percent of Zeien's work hours are spent on the development of new products.

Gillette also believes that managing hundreds of growth projects means managing hundreds of growth leaders. Zeien estimates that he personally reviews over 800 career plans for Gillette people in a 12-month period.

The dedication of much of the CEO's time to product and people development doesn't leave many hours for the balance of the job. Finance, budgets, outside activities, and a host of other responsibilities must be delegated or somehow cleared off the CEO's desk. This suggests that the process of organizational alignment must begin at the top, with a radical restructuring of CEO priorities, if new product development is to be a major growth strategy.

Zeien's practices may not be suitable for all companies, but we are seeing a new set of top management priorities emerging among product development leaders:

- Targeting opportunities for growth through new products and services, and bringing diverse talents to bear on them
- Choosing and managing platforms and technologies with the greatest potential impact on the company's future
- Viewing the stream of new product development projects as a whole, and making the difficult choices as to how resources will be allocated
- Tracking performance across projects on the measures that really matter
- Identifying and nurturing product development leaders

An aggressive strategy of new product and service development has fueled the growth engines of a substantial number of very successful companies. We have mentioned just a few. The ingredients for success in this area, however, are neither simple nor easy. If anything, new product leaders are advancing so rapidly that this strategy is becoming progressively more difficult to adopt and pursue. The opportunity for growth through new products is so great, however, that no company that aspires to greatness can afford to ignore this strategy for growth.

Our next chapter examines the possibilities for selling existing products and services in new ways and in new places: the strategy of channel management.

6

CHANNEL MANAGEMENT

✳

In 1893, John Sears hit upon an idea that created one of the greatest business success stories in American history. He developed a mail-order catalog to bring thousands of manufactured products to farmers and small-town dwellers who, until then, had limited access to the nation's growing industrial output. In a stroke, Sears' catalog gave the mining family on Minnesota's Iron Range, the farmer in Nebraska, and the bank clerk in Akron access to as many or more factory-made goods as residents of the big eastern cities.

Sears did this by creating a new distribution channel.

In a high-tech age, it's easy to become fixated on the amazing and useful new products that come out every month, while ignoring the importance of identifying the best approaches to connecting customers with these products. Cellular phones provide instant communication anywhere we go, laptop computers are now so compact and elegantly designed that we can carry tremendous computing power in a briefcase . . . and on and on.

As we've seen in the previous chapter, products like these can be the basis for powerful growth. But carving out the best ways to get products to customers is no less powerful. John Sears didn't know how to make things. His talent was selling things, and his company did this by creating a conduit between the people who made products and those who wanted them. And from this, Sears Roebuck & Company built a remarkable growth machine. In today's customer-driven economy, effectiveness at delivering products and services to customers is even more essential for prosperity and growth.

To grow, companies must sell more, either through their existing channels or through new ones. In our experience, the winners in the channel game do one or a number of things very well. They understand the needs of unique customer segments and match channel capabilities to those needs. (This may involve the use of multiple channels.) They lower the cost of delivery on an ongoing basis and they create partnerships in those steps of the value chain where other organizations can perform more effectively.

In this chapter, we present examples of companies that have created growth through effective management of their sales channels. We have divided these companies into three main camps: innovators who carve out new channels between producers and customers; companies that literally *become* the channel, and in so doing capture the most profitable value-adding activities; and companies that simply become more effective in their established channels.

Finally, we offer approaches to developing the right channels strategy. Here we develop strategy in terms of the value chain for the business, showing how different channels and various participants can work together to maximize value for different customer segments.

THE CHANNEL INNOVATORS

From retailing to transportation to health care, the variety of new channels is growing. This phenomenon has provided opportunities for some very successful companies. Starbucks (Corp.) is one example, having demonstrated how channel innovation can create remarkable growth around what most would concede is a commonplace product.

From a 1962 peak in per capita consumption, coffee was on the decline as the American beverage of choice. The traditional coffee break was gradually giving way to cola breaks, as a generation that had grown up on soda entered the work force. A spate of contradictory research reports about the medical consequences of coffee consumption had also created confusion in the public mind.

Except for the tiny niche enjoyed by gourmet coffee packagers, coffee as a product had become little more than a canned grocery store commodity. Coffee bars were few and far between, existing in only a few bohemian neighborhoods and up-scale locations.

Enter Starbucks. Starting with a bean roasting operation and a few coffee bars in the Seattle area, Starbucks changed U.S. coffee-buying habits by reinventing both the product and its distribution. Starbucks and a handful of competitors like Boston-based Coffee Connection presented coffee as a high-quality drink for discriminating consumers. Various roasts and blends of beans from exotic locations were used to differentiate the product from the feature-less, supermarket item people were used to. High standards of freshness, expert roasting, and well-trained employees made it possible to charge premium prices. Between 1987 and late 1994, the company expanded from nine Seattle-area stores to more than 425 locations around the country. In that same period, revenues grew from $1.3 million to $285 million. Profits grew apace.

Channels are central to this success story. Starbucks used a range of convenient channels—stand-alone stores, kiosks in Barnes & Noble bookstores and airport terminals, direct-mail catalogs, superior restaurants, and the specialty food sections of Nordstrom's department stores—to get its beans and brewed product to buyers. Every channel served a larger strategy: to enhance brand familiarity and brand preference. More important, the company treated its channels as an integrated network, orchestrating them to work in concert to spur growth. For example, whenever its information system spotted dense pockets of direct-mail sales, these became potential locations for new stores.

In the future, we will not be surprised to see Starbucks use brand awareness to enter the original channel for coffee sales—the supermarket shelf—attacking the traditional coffee brands in their last bastion.

Dell Computer likewise grew through channel innovation. When founder Michael Dell was still in college, personal computers were sold either through specialized computer stores that marked up prices 25 to 30 percent, or through face-to-face sales to large corporate accounts. Only a few low-end models were distributed through major department stores. This made sense when PCs were new and mysterious to just about everyone. Most customers were first-time buyers and needed the advice and counsel of salespeople—anyone, really—who could help them make the right decisions about hardware, software, and peripherals.

By the time Dell got into the business in 1984, there were lots of savvy customers around—people who already used computers at home or at the office, and who didn't need the hand-holding of dealer salespeople. What's more, this group of people was growing fast. Also, most personal computing had become standardized around common designs. The once exotic PC had become much more of a uniform set of modular elements—disk drive, memory units, monitor, keyboard, and so forth—that could be built or bought off the shelf, assembled, and sold to consumers. Operating and applications software had also become fairly standard, and part of the modular package.

The modular nature of the PC created a ready-made opportunity for "mass customization"—the creation of individually tailored products at next to mass production prices. The producer could assemble to order by finding out exactly what the customer wanted:

- How many megabytes of RAM do you need for your applications?
- What size hard drive?
- Do you want a 14- or 16-inch monitor?
- How many disk drives?
- Do you want the machine preloaded with Lotus 1-2-3 and WordPerfect, or something else?
- If you don't know, then tell us how you plan to use the machines and we'll make some suggestions.

And so forth.

The PC-maker that knew the answers to each of these questions could configure each machine for each customer, thereby adding value and gaining competitive advantage in a crowded field. Companies that did not know the answers had to build and ship PCs in different configurations to dealers, and let them sort things out with the customers.

Michael Dell made it his business to know the answers and thereby gained a competitive advantage. His company did this by creating a direct sales channel to customers through phone ordering. Its telephone staffers were far more than mere order takers. Supported by information systems that provided extensive product information keyed to the company's catalogs and advertisements, they functioned as computer consultants to all types of customers, from novices to experts. Dialogue between customers and these highly trained customer service personnel created machine specifications that could be built, shipped, and received anywhere in the continental United States in less than one week. Opening the box from Dell, the buyer found a machine that was custom-built to his or her needs, along with the right peripherals, the right applications software, and a complete set of instructions.

To better understand Dell's channel to its customers and what the value chain of activities represents, consider Figure 6–1. Dell's value chain begins with manufacturing and ends with post-sale support. (The value chain, if you are not familiar with the concept, is all the work that must be done to create and deliver value to customers.) A full-service computer dealer could handle each link in this chain *after* the point of manufacture—creating all the higher value-added functions between the factory and the customer. That's what MicroAge Computers, a very well-managed retail chain, does. Another dealer might take only the middle links, assigning delivery and post-sales support to a firm with special competence in those areas. Dell, in fact, has outsourced all responsibility for shipping to Roadway Logistics Systems. Under a recent agreement, Roadway manages and tracks all inbound and outbound shipments for the computer maker in the United States, Europe, and Asia. This is no small part of the Dell value chain; in 1995, Dell attributed 40 percent of its product costs to logistics.[1] By bringing in a "partner" with skill superior to its own in that link of the value chain, Dell expects to reduce costs and create superior economic and service value for its customers.

Channel Management

A manufacturer, in some instances, may choose to control the links that relate to large corporate accounts, leaving individual customers to a dealer network. With the exception of outside vendors that fulfill Dell's orders for some of its products, Dell covers the entire channel.

Control of manufacturing gives Dell a firm grip on its quality and product innovation. Control of subsequent links assures capture of relevant information about the customer: income and occupational characteristics; how the computer is configured (hardware and software); and how the computer is being used. This customer information provides tremendous opportunities for continuing sales. For example, when technical upgrades for hardware or software become available, the company knows exactly which of its customers are likely to benefit.

Direct-mail selling is likewise improved when coupled with a rich stream of customer information. This close link to the customer has contributed to Dell's success. And that success has been truly remarkable. The company has increased its revenues from $100 million to almost $3 billion over the past seven years by selling personal computers through direct marketing, bypassing the well-established but higher-cost dealer channels. The success of Dell's channel strategy is apparent not only in the firm's growth rate, but also in the way most of its competitors—AST, Compaq, DEC, IBM, and new start-ups—have tried to develop their own direct marketing channels.

Even this master of the single-channel strategy, however, has recognized the limits of working exclusively through direct selling. Some computer users are simply not comfortable buying through

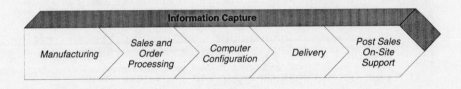

Figure 6–1. Dell Computer's Value Chain
Source: Mercer Management Consulting analysis.

direct mail. To reach these potential customers, Dell signed distribution agreements with retail merchandisers like CompUSA and Sam's Club in 1991. Four years later, these agreements were all scrapped, indicating the difficulty of branching out from a familiar channel into one where your company is a latecomer.

WHEN A COMPANY BECOMES THE CHANNEL

The most striking phenomenon associated with the changes taking place in channels is the degree to which value-added business has flowed away from the factory and toward the point of customer contact. More and more customer dollars are ending up in the hands of the companies that control the channel; fewer and fewer are finding their way back to manufacturers. For many industries, *the real money is in the channel.*

Figure 6–2 indicates this trend for the computer industry over the period 1982–1992. In terms of both end-user price and distribution of earnings, there has been a tremendous shift in favor of nonmanufacturing value-added activities. This explains why companies like Dell make a strategic choice to move beyond manufacturing, and to control the more valuable territory in the value chain traditionally provided by dealers.

This shift in value-added business from the manufacturers to the channels is particularly visible and potent among the "superstores" or "category killers"—Circuit City in consumer electronics, Home Depot in building supplies, Toys 'Я' Us in toys, and Staples and Office Depot in office supplies. Far from being traditional retailers that simply buy from wholesalers and mark up their prices, these companies create the link between manufacturers and final customers. In effect, they *become* the channel. This has given them enormous power over their suppliers and has put them in a position to provide low prices to customers.

The phenomenon is not limited to consumer products. W.W. Grainger and other industrial distributors are growing rapidly.

The so-called category killers provide some of the great growth stories of the past decade. Staples is a case in point. Staples opened

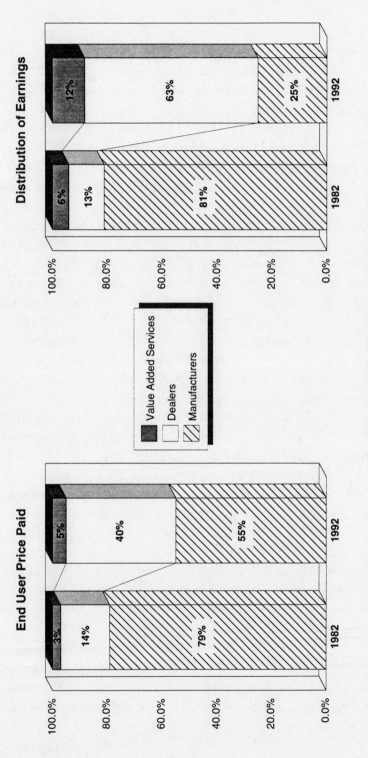

Figure 6–2. Channels Control an Increasing Portion of Value-Added Services in the Computer Industry

Source: Mercer Management Consulting analysis.

its first store in Brighton, Mass., in 1986. It took weeks to lure the first few dozen shoppers through the front door. By 1989, however, Staples had stores scattered throughout the northeastern states and sales totaling $182 million. By 1994, sales had soared to $2 billion.

Thomas Stemberg, founder of Staples, had been an executive for a grocery supermarket chain, a business built on the efficient sale of massive volumes of stock to a large number of customers at very low prices. Stemberg's innovation was in applying the food supermarket model to office supplies, office electronics, and office furniture.

Despite the fact that these goods were actually much easier to sell in mass quantity than groceries (because they don't spoil and don't have to be refrigerated, for example), they continued to be sold in small corner stores or in small departments within large department stores. When Stemberg looked at office products retailing, he found what Staples' 1993 annual report called "a highly fragmented industry characterized by numerous small and high-cost traditional dealers as well as a variety of other dealers who participated in the product category as a minor part of their total business. Traditional dealers sourced most of their product from one or two layers of wholesalers who, in turn, added price markup upon markup. As a result, the ultimate retail consumers were presented with a limited assortment of products, modest in-stock position, and high prices."

To Stemberg, this spelled opportunity. Even without experience in office supplies, he was able to see a new model for distribution. He invented an office supply superstore with all the characteristics of a supermarket. Today, Staples' operation represents a dramatic change from traditional office product retailing. Staples sources its goods directly from the manufacturers, eliminating the middlemen and their markups. Staples reinvented the channel and, in the process, provided an extraordinary pathway to growth.

Having mastered the superstore channel, Staples has now branched out to smaller Staples Express stores in downtown locations, a Staples Direct telemarketing business, and contract stationers that stock the company's on-site supply closets. Through acquisition and joint venture, the firm is growing in Canada and Europe.

With scale and a revolutionized value chain, Staples has had a dramatic impact on consumer value. Consider this statement from the company's 1993 Annual Report: ". . . in 1986, a case of copy paper typically sold for $75.00 in a retail stationery store; today at Staples, our typical retail price for quality copy paper is $19.99." Important, but left unsaid, is the impact of this pricing on competitors that cannot match Staples' economics.

LOST IN THE CHANNEL

It is always encouraging to learn about companies like Staples, Dell, Starbucks, and others that have enjoyed success through innovation. Unfortunately, as management consultants, we are more likely to see companies that are stumbling. Many have channels problems. More than a few are manufacturers who find themselves on the short end of the value-added picture described in Figure 6–2. If they have lost control of the channel between themselves and end users of their products—as in the case of some suppliers to Staples, Wal-Mart, or similar operators—then they have been cut out of the more profitable parts of the value chain.

These companies face another problem. Having ceded the conduit that links them to end users, they can no longer answer the important questions that any business with a bright future should know: Who is buying our products? How are they using our products? How do they want us to improve them? The manufacturer that simply sells into a pipeline controlled by Wal-Mart or some other channel meister has to rely on warranty card information and market research to answer these important questions. Neither is an adequate substitute for repeated and direct customer contact. And neither creates a dialogue between producer and buyer.

For these companies, the channel is like a black hole that sucks in all the important information that vendors need to understand their customers and improve their products. Trade book publishers, for example, have essentially ceded the channel for their products to wholesalers, bookstore chains, and book clubs. These organizations, and not the publishers, know the customers, and know what is being purchased, and for what purpose.

Successful companies capture and use the information found in the channel; unsuccessful companies do not.

Some companies suffer because they have been cut out of their channels, others stumble because they become hostage to them. They are in "channel prison."

Consider *Encyclopedia Britannica,* a 225-year-old publisher with one of the most respected brand names in the English-speaking world. Owned by a charitable foundation, Britannica's matchless product was sold by a direct sales force, whose power within the organization effectively blocked product innovation and alternative channels of distribution.

As recently as 1990, Britannica netted $40 million on revenues of $650 million. Those revenues were produced by 2,300 commission salespeople who earned approximately $300 every time they found someone with five feet of shelf space and $1,500 to fork over for the world's most authoritative fount of knowledge. Today Britannica still has the best encylopedia, but it is now profitless and more than half of its salespeople are gone. By 1995, revenues had dropped to $453 million and profits had given way to major losses. Its management admitted that if new capital was not found, the company would have to be sold.[2] The big sales now go to Compton's, Grolier's and Encarta, whose encyclopedias are selling briskly on CD-ROMs for between $99 and $395 through direct-mail catalogs and computer stores. Many are packaged with multimedia computer hardware.

Britannica had every opportunity to put its 44-million-word opus on CD-ROM but, according to former Britannica executives, the company's powerful sales force was dead set against a new format. Britannica was not unfamiliar with compact disk technology. In fact, it owned Compton's, a low-end encyclopedia publisher, and actually issued a CD-ROM version of its encyclopedia in 1989. Although the electronic Compton's was an instant hit, cash-strapped Britannica sold the entire operation.

Retail bankers may be the next group to be shaken by change in the channels game. In October 1994, Microsoft Corporation, the giant software company, announced plans to acquire Intuit Inc., the leading U.S. publisher of software for personal financial management and electronic bill paying. This acquisition, combined with Microsoft's plan to introduce its own on-line network for personal computers, would have made it possible for individuals to conduct many—if not most—financial transactions through their personal computers, leaving bankers out in the cold.[3] It is easy to imagine alliances between Microsoft and Visa and some major bank—each alliance being structured to fill a missing link in the total banking value chain. These would extend the range of banking services available to on-line users, and cut even more deeply into the profit-making activities of retail banks.

The Intuit deal was never consummated due to threatened Justice Department action. Just how far software companies will venture into the field of banking remains unclear. Their activities, however, underscore the role of channel innovation in reshaping the face of modern business.

THE AFFINITY CHANNEL

So-called affinity groups represent a new and potentially profitable approach to market segmentation with unique channel characteristics.

Affinity groups are clusters of customers who share some common bond: members of frequent-flyer clubs, religious groups, retired persons, and so forth. Today, companies have the marketing potential to develop products and channels for specific affinity groups. USAA, as we've already seen, has built an entire business on one affinity group—military officers. MBNA, one of the fastest growing banks in the United States, has built its business around marketing credit cards and other financial services through affinity groups.

There are also some very successful companies, such as C.U.C. International, that create their own affinity groups. Whether it is called affinity marketing or just discounting, C.U.C. sells almost $4 billion a year of merchandise and other services such as travel to

34 million "members" of its buying services. In early 1995, the stock market valued the company at over $4 billion.[4]

BEING MORE EFFECTIVE IN EXISTING CHANNELS

For every company that grows through channel innovation, dozens of others grow and prosper by becoming more effective within their traditional channels. For these companies, the right channel choices have already been made; they simply make the most of them. Paychex is one such company, and its effectiveness in its chosen channel has put it on *Forbes* magazine's list of America's best small companies and *Financial World*'s "200 Best Growth Companies."

Paychex, a $224 million company with headquarters in Rochester, N.Y., is in the payroll processing business, serving primarily small businesses. It got its start in the early 1970s by offering affordable payroll services to small businesses. Its continued focus on this underserved segment has made it the nation's second-largest payroll processor.

Small business payroll processing is a business with thin profit margins—a function of the high cost of selling the service. Just about everyone in Paychex's part of the industry has salespeople phoning and knocking on the doors of business owners, trying to win the right to do all the payroll and tax withholding that these customers must either outsource or do themselves. This sales process is expensive, and can easily absorb 50 to 60 percent of the annual value of a contract with a small company.[5] That's a major impediment to profits. Unable to find a more profitable and effective channel for reaching this customer population, Paychex simply concentrated on improving the effectiveness of its existing sales force.

Beginning in the late 1970s, the company began a process aimed at lowering selling costs by improving its sales "closing rate." The primary tool for this improvement was to establish relationships with the CPAs who handle the books and the taxes for small business owners—Paychex's target customers. Few of these CPAs have any interest in handling their clients' payrolls, yet virtually all have an interest in their clients having well-managed payroll and with-holding processes.

By selling the effectiveness of its services to these CPAs, Paychex made them a source of high-quality referrals. Before long, over 40 percent of its leads came from these CPA referrals, and a remarkable 60 percent of these became Paychex customers. More recently, a similar but fee-based referral relationship was developed with commercial bankers.[6] Today, the Paychex sales force has a closing rate roughly *ten times* higher than its nearest competitor. That level of sales productivity has both ensured a high level of revenue growth and dramatically lowered the company's cost of selling. The result: profitable growth.

Virtually every company can, like Paychex, find ways to improve the effectiveness of its existing channels.

GEOGRAPHIC EXPANSION AS A "NEW CHANNEL"

Sometimes a company has only to look outside of its home turf to generate growth by providing similar value propositions with similar operations in new territory. Companies like Nike, PepsiCo, and Microsoft have discovered and mastered geographical expansion, reaping the reward in international revenue growth of 25 percent or greater in the last five years.

Conquering the rest of the world would seem both easy and rewarding. Our colleague Nate Lentz, intrigued by the well-publicized success stories of international expansion, conducted an indepth study of the benefits of using this channel to fuel growth. He analyzed the revenue and operating profit growth rates for the Fortune 1000 companies that reported significant international operations. His research has important implications for today's managers. As Figure 6–3 indicates, companies that enjoy profitable domestic growth are able to successfully transfer that success to other parts of the world. By contrast, for companies that are experiencing problems domestically, the additional stress of expansion only exacerbates these difficulties.

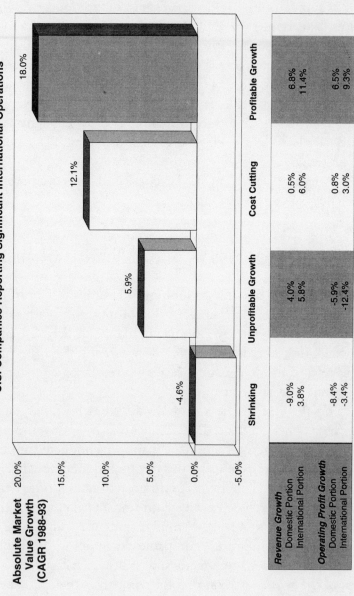

Figure 6–3. International Company Revenue and Operating Profit Growth

Source: Fortune 1000, Mercer Management Consulting analysis.

International growth is not a panacea for a stagnant company. It rewards only those who have perfected the essential ingredients of strategy design, execution, and organizational alignment at home.

GETTING CHANNEL STRATEGY RIGHT

Clearly, choosing the right channels and managing them effectively can be a strategy for growth and competitive advantage. To do so, you must:

- Understand the sources of change affecting channel decisions
- Develop strategies that match channel capabilities to supplier and customer needs
- Excel at execution

Let's look at each in detail.

The sources of change

Selecting the right channel or mix of channels is becoming more complex as the number of channels increases and their relative costs shift. Traditional channels are being supplemented, if not challenged, by newer, more technologically advanced, and often more convenient channels for the customer. As people have become more pressed for time, their trips to the shopping mall have abated. As a result, they are moving in ever greater numbers toward what they see as more convenient channels—telemarketing, direct-response advertising, on-line services, and home-shopping television networks. Direct marketing sales in the United States alone have grown at a 40 to 50 percent annual clip over the last five years, as the number of purchasers and the amount of the average purchase have both increased sharply.

The proliferation of home computers is fueling an increase in computer shopping and information gathering. One harbinger of this trend is the growth of America Online, which doubled its subscriptions in a five-month period during 1993.

Channel economics are changing along with these buying patterns. The cost of selling through direct sales forces, for example, continues to rise. The cost of an average industrial sales call jumped 40 percent in real dollars between 1984 and 1994—while the cost of electronic channels has continued to fall, making them economically viable for the first time. So, just as customers are becoming more comfortable with the new channels, the economics of these channels are becoming more attractive to suppliers.

Also changing is the role of the channel in delivering products and information to the customer. Channels are more than simple conduits for soliciting orders and delivering goods. As we have seen, for each customer–product combination there is a sales and service process—a value chain of activities—for creating awareness of the product, disseminating product information, collecting customer information, and selling, delivering, and servicing the product. In each chain, supplier, channel, and customer all play important roles. Over time, those roles become increasingly specialized, with different players taking control of different links in the chain. In a typical large-account sale in the personal computer business, for example, several players are involved. A dealer typically sells the customer one of the several computer brands it offers. A financial services company finances the transaction. A distributor stores, assembles, and ships the product to the customer.

Developing a channel strategy

In this chapter, we have presented examples of several highly successful channel strategies. In each case, the strategy created value for all participants. In addition, each strategy was sufficiently flexible to respond to changes in consumer preferences, competition, technology, and economics. Channel strategy is no longer something a company can simply "set and forget." Dell had a successful direct sales channel, but eventually felt the need to reach other customers through mass market retailers. Starbucks branched out widely beyond its original coffee shop channel.

Successful channel players recognize that each type of channel offers unique strengths and weaknesses. With this understanding, they build their strategies on two foundations:

1. *Segmentation.* Segmentation entails matching the most attractive customer segments with the channels best suited to meeting their needs.
2. *Unbundling.* Unbundling entails using different channels to fulfill different components of the value chain; one channel, for example, might be used to raise awareness of the product (through persuasion selling), another to take and fulfill the orders (through distributors), and another to service the product (through a contract service).

Segmentation and unbundling, in combination, have led to multichannel networks, whereby different players fill specific components of the value chain in a way that best meets each targeted customer segment's needs.

To do this for your company, look at your own value chain and the customer segments you serve. Align the segments with the channels that are most effective in serving them. Then identify the channel activities that you can do *very* well. If you cannot do something well, join with suppliers or partners who can handle them *very* well. Then find a way to make all the activities work in harmony.

Consider two examples. Fidelity Investments is the world's largest mutual fund company. It built its business on direct marketing skills. This single channel was a low-cost system for meeting the needs of its targeted customer segment—the self-sufficient, convenience-oriented investor. As Fidelity branched out to more customer segments, however, it had to consider alternative channel strategies. One attractive new segment was community banking customers. These individuals had the same propensity for mutual fund investing as Fidelity's but were uncomfortable with using direct-response channels. Much more hand-holding was necessary. Fidelity had an extensive product line but lacked hand-holding capabilities. Community banks, on the other hand, had plenty of financial counseling capabilities, but lacked investment products.

Fidelity and the banks are now forging partnerships whereby the bank branches serve as a new channel for Fidelity funds. This strategy delivers value to all value-chain participants—Fidelity, the banks, and the customer. Figure 6–4 is an overview of Fidelity's segmented channel network, which even includes an interactive electronic channel between Fidelity and the personal computers of its customers—On-Line Express.

H&R Block, the tax preparation service, provides another instructive example. Block prepares one in ten U.S. tax returns, primarily serving lower- and middle-income consumers. In the past, the company sold its services almost exclusively through a single channel—its network of H&R Block outlets. To better reach its targeted customers, however, Block has begun using additional channels. Nearly 10 percent of Block's tax preparation business now comes through partnerships with mass market retailers, the most significant being Sears. During the January to April tax season, Block tax preparers set up shop at kiosks inside Sears stores. In exchange for space and joint advertising, Block pays a commission on each dollar of business generated through the outlet.

This system, again, provides value to all the parties involved. For Block, it provides a new and powerful method of reaching the targeted customer. And, because most Block tax preparers are part-time staff employed only during the tax season, the seasonal kiosks allow the firm to maximize its staff utilization and minimize its fixed costs. Customers, for their part, have the benefit of convenient access to H&R Block services.

For Sears, the arrangement broadens its product set, adding revenue during a traditionally slow season. This arrangement stands in sharp contrast to an earlier co-location strategy, in which Sears attempted to sell the products of its financial services companies—insurer Allstate, investment broker Dean Witter, and real-estate broker Coldwell Banker—through its store network. This endeavor met with limited success. Segment fit explains, at least in part, the different results of the two strategies. Traditional Sears customers tend to have limited discretionary income, making them poor prospects for Dean Witter's brokerage service. (Eventually, in April 1995, Sears' shareholders approved a plan to spin off Allstate as an

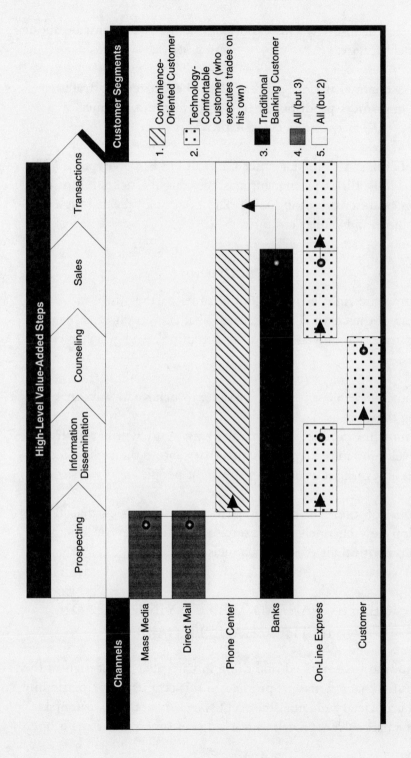

Figure 6–4. Fidelity's Channel Network
Source: Mercer Management Consulting analysis.

independent insurer.) This experience suggests an iron rule about channel strategy:

> **A channel is only successful to the degree it attracts customers predisposed to purchasing the product or service it provides.**

As Thomas M. Bloch, former CEO of H&R Block, put it, "The Sears–H&R Block partnership has been highly successful for both parties; Sears' co-location has worked because of [Sears'] high traffic volume and similar customer base."

Execution

Selecting the right channels and channel partners is by no means the end of the channel management challenge. A channel management strategy is only as good as its execution. And good execution means:

- Motivating everyone in the channel to behave in ways that support the strategy
- Minimizing conflict and maximizing synergy within the channel
- Developing information systems that capture the right information and make it available to the right people

None of these is easy. In particular, companies that try to develop new channels must exercise care that they do not create conflicts with their existing channels.

GETTING AHEAD AND STAYING AHEAD IN THE CHANNEL GAME

You should have noticed one thing in particular about each of the successful channel masters profiled in this chapter: not a single one has a proprietary channels concept. There is nothing "patentable" about a particular approach to reaching customers. Each one is open to imitation—and that imitation is well under way. Starbucks' success has inspired rival Brothers Gourmet Products and the Marriott Corporation to plan a similar chain of coffee shops. Dell's rising fortunes prompted upstart Northgate Computer Corp. to clone its direct-sales model. IBM and Compaq are doing the same. By 1995, Northgate was challenging Dell in computer shipments.

In office supplies, Staples is no longer the sole office supermarket, but faces rivals like Office Depot and Office Max, prompting Tom Stemberg to comment, "We will win only because we have better execution, not because there's this huge wall that keeps other people out of the industry."[7]

Still, first movers enjoy important advantages, not the least of which is the fact that their established competitors are to some extent in "channel prison"—bound to their current channels by infrastructure investments, dealer agreements, and other entanglements. Breaking free of these entanglements is difficult and takes time. Meanwhile, the innovators are perfecting their game—improving their information systems, building relationships with channel partners, and learning from customers. Once they get ahead on the learning curve, they're hard to catch.

So what should executives of established companies do about their channels? Two things. First, think about the strategic importance of your channels. They can be as essential to growth as your products. Second, think tactically about ways to improve existing channels or to create new ones. Here are just a few suggestions:

- *Work to understand the potential for new channels.* The earlier a company begins to experiment with new channel opportunities—the Internet, for example—the sooner management will learn about its true potential and what is required to succeed.
- *Look abroad for inspiration.* Starbucks' channel strategy was based upon its founder's experience in Italy, where he observed the popularity of coffee specialty shops.
- *Look abroad for opportunities.* Many countries have remarkably inefficient and unimaginative distribution channnels. Your domestic channel strategy may have tremendous potential for making an impact in those countries.

- *Watch your upstart competitors.* Most new challengers lack the resources to compete directly in your channels. Their best hope is to outflank you with channel innovation. This makes them extremely dangerous as they may invent the virus that kills your business. Watch these companies. If they find a successful channel play, be prepared to imitate them quickly. Don't give them four years to become entrenched—as Dell's competitors did.
- *Improve the parts of the channel that affect the total customer experience.* Auto manufacturers, in particular Saturn and Lexus, have realized that, even though they don't own their dealers, they must work to ensure that these dealers provide the best possible experience.
- *Respect but don't fear the unknown.* Moving into new channels may require new knowledge, new competencies. Many companies, for example, don't feel comfortable in retailing. Although new areas often require new competencies and involve risk, the risk of ignoring channel opportunities may be greater.

Channels are an overlooked source of profitable growth. By finding more effective channels—or just improving the ones we have—growth can be enhanced.

7

GROWTH FOUNDATIONS

✳

Each of the strategies described in the previous three chapters represents a distinctive approach to doing business. In the right hands, each can be a powerful pathway to growth. Our study of high-growth companies and our experience with clients, however, indicate that firms must do three things very well for any of these strategies to bear fruit and for growth to occur. These three things, which we call the "foundations for growth," are:

- The value proposition
- Economics across the value chain
- Execution

These are the mechanisms for facilitating strategy. Each is explained in the following sections. Despite their separate treatment in this chapter, they are actually closely bound together and interact in dynamic ways.

It is difficult to overemphasize the importance of these growth foundations. Strategies are important, but without the ability to carry them forward, strategies are sterile. Furthermore, strategies are to some extent "situationally appropriate." For example, the importance of channel management as a strategy is on the ascendancy in our current business climate, but within ten years this may no longer be the case. Acquisitions is yet another growth strategy that passes in and out of favor depending on interest rates, stock valuations, and other circumstances. The point is that though strategies may come and go, a superior value proposition, superior economics across the value chain, and an organization designed and motivated to execute well are perennial requirements for sustained growth and prosperity.

Value, value chain economics, and execution are terms used a great deal in contemporary business, but often with different meanings. Here, we define them in detail.

THE VALUE PROPOSITION

Our first foundation is *competitively superior value as perceived by customers.* Every part of this phrase is important. *Competitively superior* because absolute standards of value do not predict customer choice. *Value as perceived* because perception is reality. *By the customer* because no internal standard of value matters if it is not shared with customers.

A company's product or service is competitively superior if, at price equality with competing products, target segments always choose it. Thus, value is defined in terms of consumer choice in a competitive context. High-growth companies offer what their customers regard as a superior value. They spend a great deal of time thinking about how to create and increase the perceived value of their products and services.

The concept of value itself is a slippery one; it is used frequently in contemporary business, but rarely with precision. "We offer our customers the best value for the money," claims one company's slogan. "When you think of us, you think of value," says another. Unfortunately, these slogans are not guides to action. A more precise definition of value is offered by Bradley T. Gale, for whom "value is simply quality, however *the customer* defines it, offered at the right price."[1] In other words, value equals quality relative to price. Quality, in this definition, is simply all the nonprice attributes of a product, including after-sale service, convenience of purchase, and brand equity. (We could easily substitute the term "perceived benefits" for "quality" in this definition, and say that value equals perceived benefits/price.) Gale's value concept is represented in Figure 7–1. Here, value has two components: quality and price. And quality, itself, has a product and a service component.

This definition of value and its component parts is more than a theoretical notion. Rubbermaid Inc. defines its own sense of value in exactly these terms. For it, value is the combination of four inseparable attributes: quality, price, service, and speed.[2] For McDonald's, value is "what you get for what you pay."[3]

The notion of value *as determined by customers* and reflected in consumer choice must be emphasized here. Early practitioners of quality methods used design specifications as the yardstick to assess the quality of their products. A camshaft or other product was rated in terms of its "conformance to standards." But who determined those standards and how important were those standards to the people who bought the final product?

Using internally generated measures of quality, companies could spend heavily on features that carried very little weight with customers, adding to the price of the product without adding perceived benefits. This is sometimes difficult for technical experts to understand. In fact, this problem afflicted Detroit's auto engineers all through the 1960s and 1970s. They thought they were making their automobiles better and better, even as customers rated these same cars progressively worse. With the benefit of hindsight, we can see that the engineers were adding more innovative features and functionalities—their definition of quality—at the very time that auto buyers were growing more concerned about reliability and "fit and finish." Not surprisingly, U.S.-made automobiles almost never made

Figure 7–1. What Is Value?
Source: Bradley T. Gale, *Managing Customer Value* (New York: The Free Press, 1994), 29. Adapted with permission.

it into the upper tiers of the J.D. Powers Associates' customer satisfaction and quality lists when they were first published in the early 1980s. Instead, Japanese autos captured almost all the top places.

The impact of customer perception of value is also seen in the credit cards wars, where it has played a decisive role. When VISA and Mastercard issuers linked their cards to airline mileage programs and so-called affinity groups, they added significant perceived value to their cards with little change in price. MBNA, one of the top-growth companies in the country, built its business on affinity groups. Today, over 2,000 groups—from college alumni to environmental groups—use its cards, each perceiving some added benefit in what would ordinarily be a generic credit card. "Affinity cards" blindsided American Express, whose value became competitively weaker in the eyes of business travelers. It has countered with its own value enhancements, including airline miles.

Measuring value

A concept like value isn't very useful unless it can be measured. Imagine owning a hotel in a major metropolitan area that has dozens of competitors within a one-mile radius. Your hotel is closer to the airport than some, but farther than others. It is more convenient to the downtown business district than some, but less convenient than others. None of the hotels in your area is quite the same in terms of amenities. Most lodgers in this area are business travelers, but there are also families with children. Room rates vary from one location to the next.

The question is, at $160 per night for a standard room, is your offer perceived as a competitively superior value?

Traditional market research has failed to offer many insights into the value of one company's offering relative to its competitors. As a result, many senior executives are beginning to lose confidence in marketing research as traditionally practiced. It is good at looking in the rearview mirror to identify sales trends, at telling us what proportion of the target population is aware of our products and whether customers prefer product X over product Y, and so forth. But this type of information is very "far from the future money," as we like to say. It doesn't bring senior managers closer to the insights they need to reach decisions or change the competitive game in their favor.

Fortunately, a new generation of research methodologies has emerged. Compared to those of the past, these truly qualify as *marketing science*. They are much more effective at measuring the customer's sense of value and the drivers of behavior. And they make it possible to answer the question facing the hotel owner. Two of these methodologies are conjoint modeling and Strategic Choice Analysis (SCA)®. These make it possible, for the first time, to gain insight into perceived value before investing in products and services.

Conjoint analysis, which first appeared in the 1970s, helps executives understand the trade-offs that customers are willing to make between alternative product features. These trade-offs—between features offered either by you or by your competitors—are at the heart of most buyer decisions. Consider a simple example in which only two dimensions of product value are considered. In this example, a commercial bank is planning to revise its menu of interest-paying deposit accounts and wants to understand customer preferences among the four possible offerings shown in Figure 7–2.

Any rational consumer will identify the lower left-hand offer of 8 percent interest with no minimum balance requirement as the best value; 4 percent interest with a $1,000 minimum balance will inevitably be viewed as offering the least value. How customers respond to the other two alternatives will tell the bank a great deal about customer preferences for higher rates and full access to all of their money. When the choices are broadened to include interest rates *between* 4 percent and 8 percent and different minimum account balances, research reveals an array of customer preferences that can guide the bank in making an optimal decision about its product offerings.

Most situations involve more than just two dimensions of choices, and these result in greater research complexity. Conjoint modeling can handle this complexity, producing intelligent answers about customer preferences. But conjoint modeling does not help determine which features and prices are the real drivers of buyer decisions in a more complex—and more realistic—competitive context. To deter-

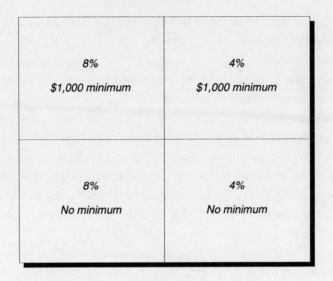

8% *$1,000 minimum*	4% *$1,000 minimum*
8% *No minimum*	4% *No minimum*

Figure 7–2. Four Bank Account Offerings
Source: Mercer Management Consulting analysis.

mine this, one must turn to Strategic Choice Analysis, a much more robust method of modeling customer choices.[4]

The intellectual history of Strategic Choice Analysis dates back to the 1960s and 1970s, when economists and psychologists at Stanford and MIT began to take on the issue of complex consumer choice. The first practical applications were in the field of public transportation—using choice analysis, economists estimated the potential demand for the Bay Area Rapid Transit and other transit systems.

SCA is a powerful tool for determining how every feature of a complex product or service contributes to the customer's perception of value. In effect, it provides the dollar value to the customer of each feature.

To understand SCA, let's return to the hotel example, using a premium hotel chain. None of this chain's hotels has exactly the same mix of amenities and location features; and because each competing hotel is likewise diverse, it is difficult to determine the customer's sense of value (price) for a night's lodging. The chain's Chicago hotel, for example, is five minutes by cab from O'Hare

Airport and 40 minutes to the downtown business district where many customers work. It has a free fitness club for guests, a "business center" with fax machines and photocopiers, a frequent traveler club, family-related amenities, and so forth. How much—in dollar terms—does each of these features contribute to (or detract from) the customer's perception of value, as determined by consumer choice? How does this value compare to that of similar hotels in the area?

The methodologies underlying SCA make it possible to answer these questions with some precision. Figure 7–3 shows what potential customers would pay for each of the aforementioned hotel features. Notice that the long drive to the downtown business district reduces the value of a night's lodging at this hotel. So does the availability of family-related amenities. Wouldn't this be worth knowing if your management team were planning to spend millions on family-amenity upgrades?

In this example, proximity to the airport is a powerful driver of customer choice, followed by the availability of a frequent traveler club. Understanding the whole and the component parts of the value proposition in this way makes it possible for decision makers to alter features and prices in ways that lead to improved profits and competitively superior value in the eyes of customers.

A major hotel chain used this methodology not long ago to determine the value proposition of its hotels throughout the world based on location factors. In many instances, those values were found to be higher than expected—so much higher that the hotel chain was able to increase its prices in many markets without damage to its occupancy rate. The result: a significant increase in profitability.

SCA also tells us a lot about price elasticity, or the sensitivity of customers to price changes. Few executives understand that different brands—whether they be of hotels or packaged foods—exhibit different price elasticities as a function of their perceived values.

By asking respondents to select from among different brands at varying price points, we can arrive at a realistic assessment of the effect of pricing changes on purchasing behavior. This helps us with pricing decisions, and indicates how demand for competitors'

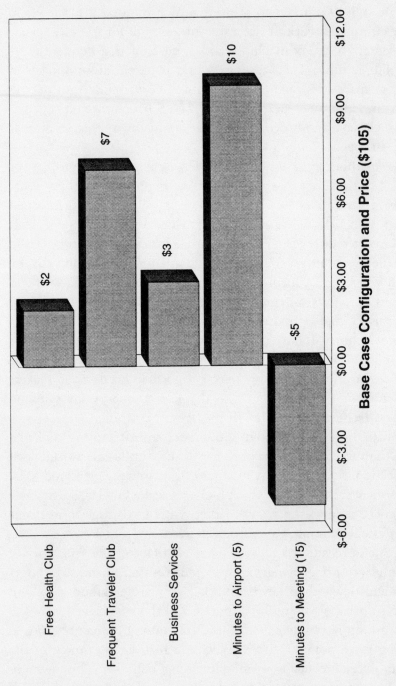

Figure 7–3. Relative Value of Various Hotel Features
Source: Mercer Management Consulting analysis.

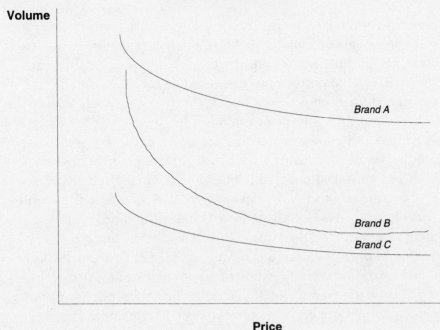

Figure 7–4. Price Elasticities of Different Brands
Source: Mercer Management Consulting analysis.

products would change if they responded to our price changes with changes of their own. In Figure 7–4, for example, we find that Brand A is the premium brand when compared to Brands B and C. Further, the slope of the demand curve indicates that demand for Brand A is not as sensitive to price changes as its nearest competitor, Brand B. So if Brand A increased its price by $1, its volume would not drop precipitously. If Brand B were to match that price increase, however, its sales volume would drop much more sharply.

Brand equity as value

The concepts of value and brand equity are closely linked. We define brand equity as the value to customers of the product quality and attributes *implied* by a brand name and reflected in their purchasing decision. Because brand equity is reflected in the choice between competing brands, it is a relative concept and can only be understood in the context of the competitive environment. While brands exist and compete daily, brand equity exists only in the mind of the customer. It can be measured only by analyzing consumer choices and teasing out price and value effects.

Brand equity is important to senior management as a corporate asset. Like other assets it must be protected, enhanced, and put to productive use. Unfortunately, we cannot manage something that is both intangible and not readily quantifiable. Until just recently, this has been the problem with brand equity. Like "value" itself, the term "brand equity" has been used loosely and without precision, and is often mixed in with the equally loose concept of "brand image."

One important extension of the new marketing science is that it gives executives an opportunity to do two things: 1) actually *measure* their brand equity, and 2) determine how perceptions of product and service quality, and even more subjective image attributes, tangibly contribute to or detract from brand equity.

Brand equity has been difficult to quantify because the prices and features of most competing products or services are never exactly the same. Nor are the messages sent to the marketplace by advertisers and marketers. Strategic Choice Analysis makes it possible to attach real numbers to this chimera. In the hotel example, we can extend our research to determine the brand equity commanded by each competing hotel chain. We do this by treating as equal all the features of all the hotels, as though all were the same distance from the airport, all had the same room rates, and so forth. Holding these features constant isolates the key variable we're looking for—the brand equity of individual competitors, which is the reason that one hotel chain can charge more than another for the same service. Figure 7–5 illustrates this concept.

Recent extensions of this methodology make it possible to identify the image perceptions surrounding these brands that account for higher or lower brand equity. And this is what gives the concept of brand management real possibilities. Some of our colleagues recently completed an exhaustive study of the brand equity of a single service brand—one of the most well-known brands in the world. This study revealed the strengths and weaknesses of the

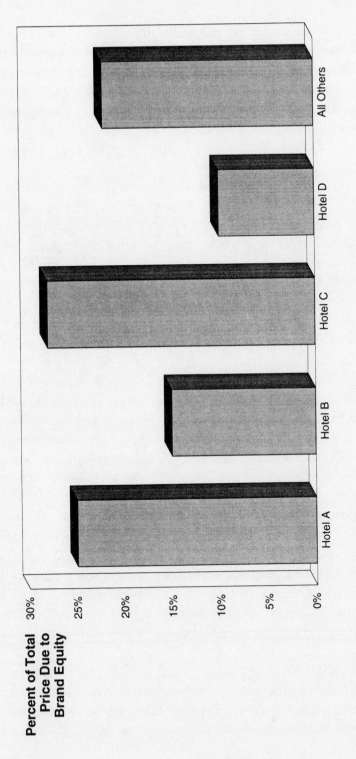

Figure 7–5. Relative Hotel Brand Equity

Source: Mercer Management Consulting analysis.

brand among customers and prospects, among more and less profitable customers, and among the target segments for new businesses. The study killed many of the company's sacred cows and
helped its leaders recognize that they had been resting on old lau-
rels in a market where the products, services, and brand equity of
competitors were increasing rapidly.

Being competitively superior

The most meaningful research results for decision makers are
obtained when we measure value not only against customer
expectations—which is typically the case—but also against what
competitors are offering. This is how we develop an understanding
of what constitutes *competitively superior value*. We've just shown
how that can be done. Remarkably, few companies attempt to figure this out. For example, every reader who travels encounters the
typical car rental questionnaire that asks, among other things: "Was
your experience at our service desk 1) poor, 2) fair, 3) good, 4) very
good, or 5) excellent?" The responses tell the car rental company
how customers feel about their experience, but they indicate nothing about how the rental firm rates relative to its universe of competitors. Even if customers overwhelmingly give the company an
"excellent" rating, its key competitors might also be rated "excellent" by those same customers. But the research would be mute on
this important point.

This example points to a fundamental problem with a business
strategy that focuses on customer satisfaction—the case with many
companies enamored of total quality management (TQM). Focusing on the concept of customer satisfaction without reference to
competitive value can be a trap. One can build quality into products beyond what the customer requires and compound this error
with costs and prices that result in overall lower value than that of
the competition's products. A good example of this is AT&T's
home telephone sets prior to the breakup of the phone company.
During the era of the telephone monopoly, AT&T and Western
Electric made the highest-quality telephone sets in the world. You
could drop them, slam them down, and use them for 30 years.

Once competition hit, AT&T had to introduce new products and, in effect, alter the durability of some of its telephones to be competitive with lower-cost and lower-priced phones that provided a higher value proposition to consumers.

In comparing value, we must also recognize that companies need to rank themselves against a market peer group—that is, against companies that serve the same market segments. For example, comparing the brand equity of Motel 6 with that of Four Seasons Hotels would be unproductive, since these two lodging chains serve consumers seeking vastly different value propositions.

Value as a moving target

All companies face the problem of being backward looking when they assess the value of their offerings. Formal research and contacts with customers indicate what customers perceive as value at a fixed point in time. But customer expectations and perceptions change, and competitors continually alter the price and quality dimensions of the value equation through their actions. These changes create a dynamic situation to which companies must respond with equal dynamism. Companies that aim to grow must be sure that their current products and services are keeping pace with changing customer expectations. And new products must represent superior value at the launch stage, not at the planning stage. Some companies have addressed this through competitive swat teams that watch—and pretend to be—the competition.

Another technique, Information Acceleration (IA)®, is a methodology for establishing future targets for value creation. This new research tool further addresses the need for marketers to estimate consumer response to new products and new product categories. Historically, short of costly field trials, companies have not had a way of determining how consumers will react to an entirely new product or service. Consumers cannot accurately gauge their response to new products if they lack awareness, knowledge, and experience with the product or service category. This was well illustrated as long ago as the 1950s, when researchers told Xerox that there would be no demand for its copier machines.

IA addresses this limitation by taking advantage of multimedia technology (video, graphics, sound, motion, and text) to condition the customers to the future, when new products will be introduced, and to provide a natural and sensory-rich research environment to test concepts.

In an IA research context, survey respondents interact with a multimedia workstation that "accelerates" information about products and services and makes that information available through simulated testimonials, advertisements, in-store displays, sales presentations, product literature, and other elements of the marketing mix. It puts survey respondents into the environment of a future marketplace. Recent applications of IA include product design and sales forecasting for multimedia services, interactive network systems, wireless communications, electric vehicles, and consumer electronics.

Because IA uses interactive multimedia, it allows an assessment not only of consumer response, but also of what elements of the marketing mix (advertising, word of mouth, etc.) have the greatest impact. This means that it is possible to use IA as the core of the marketing strategy. In other words, not only does IA provide a reliable forecast, it also gives management the tools with which to develop effective marketing strategies that meet those forecasts. Currently, no other approach—except for expensive, inflexible, and time-consuming field trials—enables a company to gather this information on fundamentally new products and services.

Industry leaders set the hurdle level for value. Companies like AT&T, GE, and Microsoft have demonstrated an ability to raise that hurdle level progressively higher—too high for competitors to reach quickly or easily. All too often, however, industry leaders either lose touch with the customers they serve or become bureaucratic and political and unable to focus on their value proposition.

ECONOMICS IN THE VALUE CHAIN

In the previous chapter, we saw how a number of companies had captured growth opportunities by identifying and filling key links in the value chain. The value chain is the whole series of events that are required to make, sell, deliver, and use a product or service.

We stress the point that it is the effectiveness of the *entire* value chain—not its individual links—that matters to customers. It is the economic sum of the individual links that the end user pays for. This leads us to the second growth foundation: *comparatively superior economics across the value chain*. Here again, all the words are important. *Comparatively superior* because each link in the value chain should be measured not only against competitors but also against "comparators"—other firms that conduct similar activities, even if their products or services are not in the same competitive arena. *Economics* because the value chain only works if it makes money. *Across the value chain* because every link, even those formerly not taken seriously, must perform a value-adding function.

In commodity industries, superior economics across the value chain is the ultimate arbiter of success and failure. The stunning growth of Nucor Corporation is a case in point.

When Nucor Corporation broke ground for its Crawfordsville, Indiana mill in 1988, this innovative company delivered yet another serious blow to competitors who rely on the traditional value chain for steel making. Practitioners of "integrated" steel making start with iron ore, coal, and limestone and process these materials through a series of very expensive machinery, coke batteries, blast furnaces, basic oxygen furnaces, and casting machines to produce a thick slab of steel.

This part of the steel-making process was a major, capital-intensive industry in its own right, but it was only the front end of the sheet steel business. Each slab had to be reheated to extremely high temperatures, then run through roughly $1 billion worth of rolling mills until it was flattened to the thickness of your car's sheet metal skin.[5] In 1988, a good mill could produce a ton of this steel at roughly $325.

Nucor's Crawfordsville "mini-mill" was designed to change this steel making process and its underlying economics, which by then was four decades old. Technical innovation was nothing new to Nucor. The company had already shown technical leadership in the use of electric arc furnaces to melt scrap steel as a replacement for the capital-intensive blast furnace process. Crawfordsville was to be a showcase for yet another bold step—the first practical application of a German technology for continuous casting. It would melt scrap steel in an electric arc furnace, then pour a continuous three-inch-thick ribbon of steel that needed minimal rolling to produce a thin sheet. For Nucor, a tiny company in an industry of giants, experimenting with the untried German technology was a tremendous gamble, but one that paid off. Once the Crawfordsville plant became operational and hit its stride, it was producing sheet steel at some $20 per ton less than its competitors.

Over the next four years, the fruits of Nucor's winning gamble were seen in generous bonuses for its workers and managers, and a company market value that grew from $1.3 billion in 1989 to $2.3 billion in 1993.

The impact of Nucor's success with continuous casting has clear parallels with process innovations in glass making, petroleum refining, the production of synthetic fibers, and many other process industries. In each case, a technological innovation fundamentally altered the economics of the industry, causing massive reductions in unit production costs. Those that created or adopted the innovations enjoyed tremendous business success; those that clung tenaciously to the old ways of doing things were swept from the field.

Perhaps the closest analogy to Nucor's innovation may be found in the continuous casting of plate glass, an achievement that Britain's Pilkington Company first introduced in the late 1950s. Pilkington spent six years developing its now universal "float process" for making plate glass. This represented the latest in a century-long train of innovations that systematically reduced the process from a long and expensive series of disconnected steps— mixing, melting, casting, annealing, grinding, and polishing—to simply mixing and melting and pouring molten glass into a continuous ribbon. Pilkington's innovation, like Nucor's, created tremendous economies: labor costs dropped by 80 percent, scrap by 30 percent, and energy consumption by 50 percent.[6] This gave

Pilkington such cost advantages that rival firms had only two options: quit the field or license the float process technology from its creator.

Pilkington and Nucor altered the value chains in their respective industries, and in so doing created superior economics for themselves and their customers. Figure 7–6 diagrams the value chains for Nucor and for its Big Steel rivals.

As seen in the previous chapter, successful companies handle those links in the value chain that they can do very well, and leave the others to partners, suppliers, or other firms that have superior capabilities in those areas. This is what Nucor did in acquiring high-quality scrap steel through suppliers. It outsourced the big front end of the steel-making business. Unlike its older, integrated competitors, it didn't invest in ore mines, ore ships, or blast furnaces. It didn't need to, as long as there was an adequate supply of good scrap steel around to feed its operations. Now the company is building a plant in Trinidad to produce iron carbide as a hedge against scrap shortages.

Within the remaining portions of the value chain, Nucor substituted traditional casting and milling with its own, economically superior process innovations. Taken as a whole, this new value chain created undeniable economic advantages for Nucor and its customers—advantages so overpowering that Nucor's sales increased 16 percent during the period 1988–1993, while the collective sales of its key rivals—USX, Inland Steel, and Bethlehem Steel—shrank by 1 percent.

Every company is part of a chain that creates value for customers. In most cases, as we see here with Nucor and as we observed in our earlier discussion of channel strategy, more than one organization is part of the chain. Following the principle of labor specialization first articulated by Adam Smith, each does what it does best in adding value. The current explosion of business alliances and "virtual" corporations simply reflects a growing recognition that few single enterprises have all the capabilities needed to complete the value chain at the greatest possible speed and at the least cost.

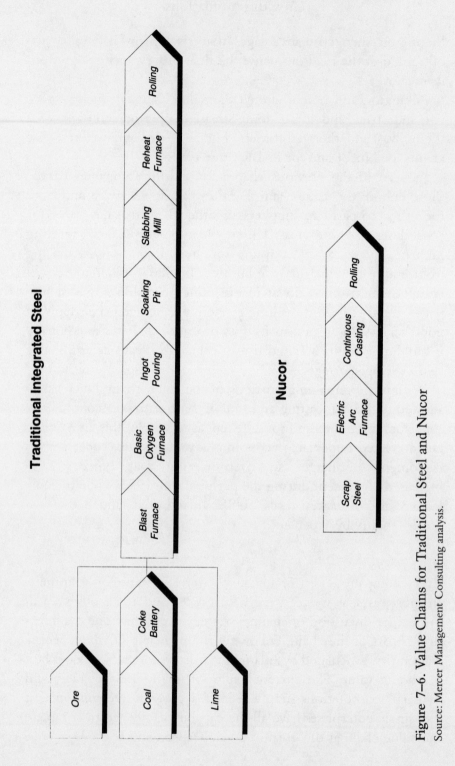

Figure 7–6. Value Chains for Traditional Steel and Nucor
Source: Mercer Management Consulting analysis.

The economics of the chain form one of the essential foundations upon which business success is gained or lost.

Improving economics in the chain

Nucor used a technological innovation—continuous casting—to create order of magnitude improvements within its value chain. Where traditional methods required four hours to produce a ton of finished sheet steel, continuous casting cut that time to just 45 minutes. The productivity of labor exploded from 450 tons per employee to 1,200. In any industry, such earth-shaking innovations are few and far between, and difficult to plan. In a century of "cracking" heavy hydrocarbons to produce gasoline, for example, truly major increases in productivity are associated with only two major innovations, and neither of these originated with the dominant companies in the industry.[7] Clearly, if executives are to improve the economic bases of their businesses, they cannot rely on breakthrough technologies.

Continuous improvement of business processes is a practical and effective approach to enhancing the economics of the value chain. Continuous improvement is simply an incremental but unending series of steps toward operational excellence, and is one of the core values of the Baldrige National Quality Award. The notion of the "experience curve," whereby unit costs drop as a producer learns and refines its production processes, is part and parcel of this concept.

Most manufacturers today understand continuous improvement, and a growing number have incorporated it into their practices. It is less often practiced among service firms, though its effectiveness over time is no less impressive in this context. USAA is one example. Through a highly coordinated set of improvements to its information systems, this insurer has increased its productivity from one employee for every 152 policies, to one employee to more than 1,000 policies today.

Truly dramatic economic improvements are made when technological innovations are combined by continuous incremental improvement. Companies that rely on breakthrough innovations are a bit like baseball teams that rely on hitting a certain number of home runs to outpace their competitors. And companies that rely on incremental improvements are like the teams that aim to hit a lot of singles and doubles. In the long run, neither strategy is sufficient, but their combination almost guarantees a winning season.

In the years since continuous casting was brought on line, for instance, Nucor has achieved further economies through incremental improvements that have made this breakthrough steel-making method more and more efficient. The coupling of a breakthrough innovation with continuous improvement produces a cost performance situation similar to that shown in Figure 7–7. Here, the level of cost performance exceeds the level that could be achieved by innovation or continuous improvement alone.

Another effective practice for improving the economics of the value chain is benchmarking. Simply defined, benchmarking involves measuring and comparing one's own business processes against those of business process leaders in any industry in order to gain information on which process improvement can be based. The goal is to bring the benchmarking company's operations to a performance level that equals or exceeds that of best-in-class companies.

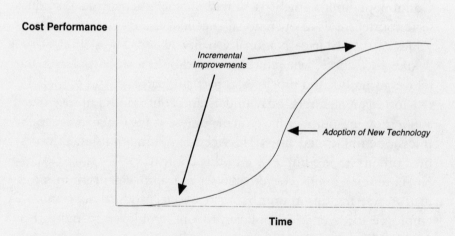

Figure 7–7. Cost Performance of New Technology Implementation and Incremental Improvements
Source: Mercer Management Consulting analysis.

Companies have been copying the best practices of their direct competitors for years. The Japanese, on the other hand, followed Deming's injunction to "adapt, not adopt," and created the foundations of the benchmarking methodology. In the United States, Xerox became the leader in this methodology, making it a cornerstone of the improvement initiative that reversed its flagging fortunes in the 1980s. A team led by Robert Camp conducted the company's landmark cross-industry benchmarking survey in 1982, with its study of L.L. Bean's approach to "picking and packing" thousands of small orders every day. Although the two companies were in totally different industries, Xerox's logistics and distribution personnel found a clear analogy in Bean's order fulfillment challenge and—more important—a superior process for meeting that challenge. Through analysis and adaptation, Xerox was able to lower costs and improve performance in its own picking and packing operations.

Today, benchmarking is used by at least 75 percent of the Fortune 500 industrial companies. It has also become a mandatory management process for Baldrige Award applicants. Many companies employ benchmarking as part of a program of continuous improvement, using it to identify what it is that they need to improve and the levels of performance to which they might aspire.

Reengineering is merely the latest of the performance improvement methods. When practiced correctly, it represents the best combination of tools for improving economics in the value chain, in part because it calls into question the structure of the existing system for creating value. Its willingness to entirely eliminate current business processes in favor of better ones creates the potential for the same kind of performance breakthrough that (as shown in Figure 7–7) technological change makes possible—i.e., great leaps in cost performance. Executed correctly, reengineering takes the customer as the focal point, and works back from there to create a chain of processes that serves that customer in the optimal way.

Reengineering is not without its problems, as the current high levels of failed or incomplete implementations attest. In many cases, however, the fault does not lie with the methodology but with the way it is used. There is now plenty of evidence that companies are using reengineering simply to cut costs—i.e., people—and not to create improvements in their core business processes.

Beyond reengineering, the ultimate form of change in the value chain is *business reinvention.* This is the creation of totally new ways to deliver products and services that make earlier value chains, no matter how well they are managed, obsolete. Nucor's mini-mill technology verges on reinvention. Other examples include the use of shipping containers that could be carried on ships, trucks, and railroad cars. Business reinvention should always be on the mind of managers as both an opportunity and a threat. Working to perfect the trim of your sails is insufficient if someone else is inventing the steamship.

EXECUTION

Execution is the third foundation for growth. A firm may have the best-designed and best-advertised products or services in its industry, but if it cannot translate design specifications into flawless products, if it cannot fill an order promptly and accurately, if its employees are unmotivated or inattentive to customers, then its hopes for growth will be unfulfilled. It will be no more successful than the football team that has a terrific game plan but cannot block, tackle, pass the ball, or summon up the will to win.

This third growth foundation demands *consistently superior strategy execution through organizational alignment. Consistently superior* because most strategies now leave no room for error. *Through organizational alignment* because the principal cause of failed execution, we are convinced, is not incompetence but operational decisions and organizational designs and practices that are in conflict with each other. In a nutshell, this means that the structure, work processes, management practices, and culture of a company all serve the creation and delivery of value to the customer.

Execution is the hardest job of all. Managers who attend our executive forums invariably point to this area as the great barrier to growth for their companies. One reason is that it pits managers against a phalanx of tough problems.

For example, how do you transform your new product development process so that 30 to 50 percent of annual revenues are from products brought to market in the last five years when there is no discernible process for developing new products, when responsibility for new product development is shared by sales, marketing, and materials development, and when no one suffers a personal income loss when market introductions are consistently delayed 12 to 18 months?

What does superior execution look like?

Consistently superior execution is like great art: you know it when you see it. You see superior execution when you walk into a McDonald's restaurant. The place is clean. The food is fresh and prepared to standards. The lines move quickly because the people behind the counter clearly know what they are doing.

Go into the kitchen and you'll see an operation in which all the activities have been thought through with care. People know what they are expected to do, and they've been given the training to do it well. Meet the franchise owner and you'll encounter someone committed to the McDonald's concept of value and success. At the corporate level, McDonald's supports this entire chain of activities with training, continuous product experimentation, and vigorous enforcement of standards.

From top to bottom, the McDonald's operation is aligned to produce the experience you had when you walked through the front door. In a world glutted with fast-food restaurants, McDonald's continues to grow because of its culture of carefully paced change, its systems that recruit, train, and motivate thousands of low-skilled workers, and so forth. The McDonald's concept is easy to imitate; its ability to execute is not.

While consistently superior execution is the result of policies and practices that take place *inside* a company, customers have no trouble seeing it from the outside. Check into a Ritz Carlton Hotel sometime and you'll understand what we mean. If you travel frequently on business, as we do, you know the frustration of bouncing around between airports, cab rides, meetings, and hotels. By the end of the day the last thing you want to do is stand in line simply to register for a room. Ritz Carlton understands this and has designed every point of customer contact and service delivery to be effortless and efficient. When you check in at a Ritz Carlton Hotel (assuming you have stayed at a Ritz previously), you don't have to fumble around for your corporate rate number. You don't have to fill out your name and address, your company's name, or do other tiresome chores. The hotel's database has taken care of these annoying steps. Do you prefer a nonsmoking room? No need to ask; the hotel already knows.

Ritz Carlton customers notice these details in execution and respond by making Ritz Carlton their choice of places to stay.

USAA customers notice too. When they call the company's San Antonio headquarters, they don't get shuffled around from extension to extension. They don't have to wait around while their files are being located. They deal with someone who can handle their inquiry on the spot. Whether they want to buy a new car, insure it, add a new person to an existing policy, or simply change address or coverage, it takes just one call to one person at USAA (and an average of five minutes) to complete the transaction.

This level of efficient service is only possible because USAA has built an information system that puts all customer policies and records on line and at the fingertips of every customer service representative. The information system is aligned with customer requirements. Equally important, the company has organized itself and trained its work force so that a very high level of service is possible. Everything is structured around USAA's customer service goal to "Do it right the first time."

Getting organization right

The superior execution just described is provided by the organization. Organization is more than just the boxes on the organization chart. It includes the work processes that the company performs, the leadership that inspires people to give their best, and the informal relationships that fill the empty spaces between the boxes. The incentives and penalties that influence behavior, and the inevitable tension between control from the top and independent action by individuals and groups, are also part of organization.

At the risk of stating the obvious, we can say that regardless of the strategy you adopt, your business must be organized in such a way that people have an incentive to do the right thing, that the right people are assigned to the right jobs, and that all of their individual efforts are channeled in the right direction. Having said this, we must tell you that our experience with senior executives indicates that building a fully aligned and motivated organization can be both mystifying and difficult. This is an area in which very little progress has been made over the years, especially when compared to the widespread understanding of customer value and economics.

Today, most companies have access to ample tools for determining what customers want now and will value in the future. Greater economies in the value chain have also been achieved in many industries. Over the past 15 years American and European corporations have discovered how quality control, just-in-time approaches to inventory, continuous improvement, benchmarking, TQM, and now reengineering can improve their microeconomies. These have been extremely potent tools for improvement, and have truly revolutionized the production of goods and services. Moreover, these tools are transferable from company to company, from one industry to another, and from manufacturing to services. Any company with sufficient dedication can master them.

Organizational issues are another story. They remain the last frontier in modern management. Here, progress in usable theory has been slow. Despite all that has been written and preached about how to lead, how to motivate, and how to structure our business organizations, it is difficult to point to tangible and *progressive* improvement in any of these categories. Further, our experience with successful companies points to no single management style, organizational structure, or motivational system that defines the ideal organization.

Despite what you may be hearing about the learning organization, horizontal management, cross-functional teams, and empowered workers, we cannot endorse a single universal principle for organizing for growth. While there are many compelling examples of companies that have improved performance by adopting one or more of these concepts, there is no "silver bullet" for universally solving organizational problems. The absence of a cure-all has not stopped managers from seeking one, which explains the succession of business improvement programs that enjoy great popularity for a few years, only to fade away.

For the most part, the quest for the "right" way to organize people and activities has centered on the issue of command and control from the top versus decentralization and participative management. The perennial tension between these philosophies of organization was first described a quarter-century ago by John Morse and Jay Lorsch, who in 1970 wrote:

> During the past 30 years, managers have been bombarded with two competing approaches to the problems of human administration and organization. The first, usually called the classical school of organization, emphasizes the need for well-established lines of authority, clearly defined jobs, and authority equal to responsibility. The second, often called the participative approach, focuses on the desirability of involving organization members in decision making so that they will be more highly motivated.[8]

So how are managers to choose between these two conflicting philosophies? Morse and Lorsch went on to review what was known about their application. What they discovered was intuitively obvious, and coincides with our own experience with advising companies in the 1990s. They found that there is no one best approach to organizing a company. Instead,

> ... the best approach depends on the nature of the work to be done. Enterprises with highly predictable tasks perform better with organizations characterized by the highly formalized procedure and management hierarchies of the classical approach. With highly uncertain tasks that require more extensive problem solving, on the other hand, organizations that are less for-

malized and emphasize self-control and member participation in decision making are more effective. In essence . . . *managers must design and develop organizations so that the organizational characteristics fit the nature of the task to be done* [our emphasis].[9]

Many would like to believe that workers in participative organizations are bound to be more motivated, but Morse and Lorsch's own research debunked this idea. They found instead that motivation can be encouraged in many ways, the best way being to *tailor the organization to fit the task and the people*. They called this "contingency theory." The right organization, then, is contingent upon the job to be done and the kind of people involved. Our observations of the organizational approaches of growing companies confirm this essential finding.

In the consistently growing companies on our list we have observed similarities in how managers create customer-perceived value and how they achieve high levels of process execution. When we look at the area of organization, however, those similarities disappear. The practices we do observe appear to be highly *contingent* upon the particular tasks at hand. We see highly decentralized companies in which goals are set and empowered employees are given a great deal of freedom in achieving them. Nucor, for example, equips worker teams in its steel mills with the right tools and strong financial incentives and gives them wide latitude in reaching a stated objective: making quality steel faster. These teams set the pace of their own work, weed out incompetents and malingerers, and find ways of doing things more efficiently than anyone could have expected. Nucor teams very often sustain machine output at twice the rated capacity.

Management at this high-growth company is content to stand back and let its work force build and run its world-beating plants. Nucor's philosophy, as articulated by Chairman F. Kenneth Iverson, is that "the average employee is one hell of a lot smarter than most corporate executives will give him credit for . . . If they really want to find some of the answers to productivity or product improvements, ask the guy who's doing it. It's that simple." That philosophy translates into remarkably few layers of management at Nucor. In fact, this company of 6,000 employees produces some $2.3 billion in revenues with a corporate headquarters of about 30 people.

We also see growing companies that are extremely structured in how work is done. McDonald's, for example, operates in highly controlled, by-the-numbers fashion. About the *last* thing it would do would be to "empower" its employees to depart from the script. It has a formula for successful operations, and adherence to the formula is expected. You won't hear a McDonald's restaurant manager tell the kitchen crew, "Here's the grill and the deep fryer—I'm empowering you to work out the best system for making hamburgers and french fries." Innovations are developed centrally.

As near as we can tell, the common organizational feature of high-growth companies has nothing to do with whether they follow a command and control approach or its opposite. There are plenty of examples of both. Despite the popularity of current management nostrums, there is no universal advantage to being a learning organization, to using cross-functional teams, or anything else. *There is no single best way for all companies.* There is, however, a single best way for each company. The executive's job is simply to create the organization that best serves the goal of profitably delivering the highest value to customers.

We believe that the most important ingredient in organizational planning is alignment. Starting with the value proposition, proceeding through an understanding of the value chain, the manager must ensure that the organization works consistently to deliver the value proposition and that the components of the organization are not at cross-purposes.

Alignment is critical

One of the worst mistakes any executive can make is to tolerate misalignment in the way jobs, incentives, and lines of authority work to deliver value to customers. A classic case of such misalignment was observed by one of the authors many years ago at a corporation that owned a chain of cookie stores. The stores were located in shopping malls and other areas of high pedestrian traffic around the United States. This chain was concerned about the great profit variability among its outlets. Some stores were very profitable and others were just the opposite, and that variability could not be explained by location, weather, store design, or other factors. Analysis, however, made it clear that the unprofitable stores all had high levels of waste. Waste in this business occurs either because stores make too many of some types of cookies or because they make types that people do not especially like. Both are under the store manager's control.

Senior executives of the cookie chain were mystified by this problem. Over the years, they had developed operating procedures that translated into a highly reliable and predictable business. These made it clear what kinds of cookies to bake, when to bake them, and in what quantities. As far as corporate executives were concerned, it was difficult to lose money as long as managers simply followed procedures. Further, store managers had clear compensation incentives to reduce waste and improve profitability. So why were some managers not creating profits?

Investigation by the consulting team found the answer not in the cookie outlets themselves, but in the human resources department of the conglomerate that owned the cookie store chain. When human resource functionaries advertised and interviewed store manager candidates, they touted the job's independence: "Be an entrepreneur. Run your own business." Interviewers looked for people with creativity and independence of judgment. Not surprisingly, most of the people they hired were not disposed to follow standard procedures for running a profitable cookie store. Many, in fact, quickly began their own experiments, making the mistakes that the chain's own procedures book would have helped them avoid. Few of these managers lasted for one year. Ironically, the new managers who met the hiring criteria less well performed better.

It never occurred to the people doing the hiring that they needed people who would work very hard in conformity with proven procedures. Instead, they tried to hire people who yearned for empowerment. The critical process of hiring was simply not aligned with how the company wanted to run its business.

This story summarizes in a simple way the complex problems that enterprises often have with aligning their organizations to deliver value to their customers. These problems are compounded in functionally organized companies when someone outside of the key business processes (human resource personnel, in this example) is involved in decision making. This is one of the reasons that the so-called horizontal organization—a systematic approach to integrating business leadership, functional expertise, and process management—is emerging as a powerful tool for creating alignment.

Stories of companies that do not grow are often awash in examples of misalignment. One business lived or died by its retention of large, long-term customer relationships but paid its customer contact personnel only for the sale of new accounts. A restaurant chain tried to compete on the strength of its "like home" cooking but saved money by hiring unskilled chefs and training them for one day. A common sign that the business is out of alignment is when it is necessary to break the rules in order to do the right thing for the business.

Getting alignment right

While there is no single best way to organize and align the activities of a company, we find that growing enterprises share a few common practices:

1. Management communicates its strategy for satisfying customers to all levels of the organization. Everyone understands that strategy and his or her part in it.
2. Leadership of the company is consistent in demonstrating support for the strategy.
3. The formal structure of the company is organized so that key customer needs are easy to meet.
4. Incentives, measurements, and accountability emphasize the acts that build customer satisfaction.
5. The major business processes are designed and managed to offer superior customer value and to operate with the best economics.

6. People are selected, trained, and motivated in ways that are consistent with the strategy.

7. The company works to foster a culture that supports the strategy and doesn't fight it.

8. There is an orientation toward change that seeks to accept its inevitability and to capitalize on the opportunities which it poses.

UNITING STRATEGY WITH THE GROWTH FOUNDATIONS

If there is no universal blueprint for organizing for growth, what are executives to do? Contingency theory and our own observations suggest that there is a natural progression to how managers should create or reform their companies. This progression is described in Figure 7–8. For any given strategy, they should determine what constitutes competitively superior value in the eyes of their customers. With this value clearly articulated, they should then develop the *means* to create and deliver it with overwhelming efficiency. That means creating superior economics in the value chain. Execution through a properly aligned organization follows. The tasks at hand determine the structure of the organization and whether directed or independent work is most appropriate. These may even coexist within the same organization. R&D, for example, may be a task in which empowered teams and horizontal work processes represent the best solutions. The assembly line may call for a different style entirely.

This linear approach to creating capabilities in support of strategy is not entirely different from the "clean sheet of paper" concept advocated by reengineering guru Michael Hammer. Under his system, a company acts as if it were starting from scratch, asking, "If this is what the customer wants, what would be the most efficient way to create and deliver it?" In developing the foundations for growth, we say, "If this is our chosen strategy for serving customers, how will we determine what they want (value), develop

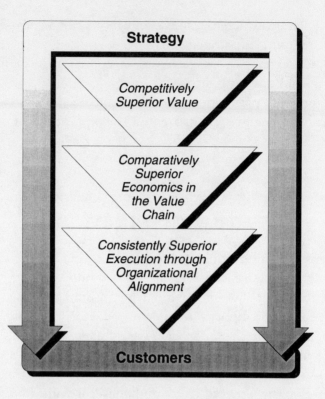

Figure 7–8. The Progression of Growth Capabilities

Source: Mercer Management Consulting analysis.

an economic system to make and deliver that value, and create the kind of organization and incentives to make it all possible?"

But executives cannot simply throw away the companies they have and start with a clean sheet of paper. Nor can they remake them overnight. Changing the structure and culture of a large organization is one of the most difficult and uncertain jobs that any executive can tackle. In many cases, it may not be necessary. Instead, you may be able to start with any one in our series of three requirements—value, economics, and execution. Acquisitions-oriented companies, for example, can acquire companies that have products and services (values) that they know how to manage. Our own parent firm, Marsh & McLennan Companies, Inc., followed this approach when it acquired its management consulting operations.

Marsh & McLennan enjoyed great success in advising large companies on matters of insurance. It had the organizational wherewithal to effectively run other high-level business advisory services—like management consulting. In effect, it acquired a new value proposition that fit well within its existing organization.

The important point about our three foundations of growth is that *they must fit together* in support of the company's chosen strategy.

8

GETTING TO GROWTH

✳

As we've seen, the great majority of America's largest companies are not experiencing substantial growth. Many have already faced the downsizer's ax, yet for them the road to growth and prosperity remains elusive.

Getting back to growth after years of no progress is never easy. For companies trying to pull themselves out of actual decline, the task is even more difficult. Turnarounds are difficult, rare, and generally short-lived. Most attempted turnarounds are launched when companies find themselves in a crisis. They muster the energy and will to deal with the crisis—usually through cost cutting or restructuring—but rarely with the fundamental issues that put them into crisis in the first place. These fundamental issues may be declining demand for their main product lines, rising customer expectations, or technological innovations developed by competitors. Cost cutting and restructuring may provide momentary relief at the bottom line, but failure to address the fundamental competitive issues causes a lapse back into crisis.

At the same time, the standards that distressed companies hope to meet are continually moving higher. Whether it's cost per ton of rolled steel, the labor hours required to assemble an automobile, the number of new successful products, or customer service levels, industry leaders are always "raising the bar" that all the others have to leap over if they want to capture customers and profits. Unfortunately, most business improvement programs fail to recognize this fact. They take the current best standards of performance as their target, but by the time they reach them the real market standards have been raised, sending them back into crisis.

It is not surprising, then, that the business landscape is littered with corpses. Companies that fall into decline more often than not continue the downward slide until they are either absorbed by another company or disappear altogether. This being the case, there is much to learn from companies that have successfully rebounded from stagnation or decline. What combination of inspiration, leadership, and technique made it possible for these companies to escape the fate that has befallen so many others? How have they managed to return to growth?

Turnarounds are rare. Of the 395 Fortune 1000 companies that we classified as Profitable Growers from 1988 to 1993, 87, or 22 percent, had two or more years of declining revenue at any time during the period 1983–1993 (see Chapter 3). This would imply that only one in five profitable growth companies reached this state through a turnaround in the last decade.

To answer these questions, we look at four companies in very different industries. Each was faced with a serious problem—declining revenues or profits, loss of market share to new challengers, lost product leadership, or simply exhausted growth opportunities within its current business. In most cases, companies faced more than one of these problems. Yet each found its way back to growth.

CORNING FINDS THE NEXT WAVE

Corning, Inc., provides an instructive model for how a large, established company can regenerate its stream of revenues and profits. From the company's founding in the mid-nineteenth century by Amory Houghton and his sons until the 1980s, its fortunes have been intimately tied to glass and related technologies. Corning's first great bonanza came in 1879, when it developed the process technology to manufacture incandescent light bulbs for the Edison Electric Company, the precursor of General Electric. That business, and products developed in its pioneering research laboratory, were to sustain Corning for one hundred years.

The company grew and prospered under several generations of

Houghtons and nonfamily managers. The post-World War II era was particularly bountiful. Between 1946 and 1961, sales quadrupled. As the major producer of the glass bulbs housing TV picture tubes, Corning was a major beneficiary of the television age. According to one company executive, "The TV business was just raining money out of the sky."[1] Over the next five years, revenues doubled again, return on equity reached 20 percent, and Corning became a Wall Street favorite, selling at an incredible 40 times earnings.

By the late 1960s, Corning sat comfortably unchallenged atop a diverse set of glass- and glass-ceramic-based businesses. But even as many business pundits and investors hailed it as an icon of American industry, Corning's glass empire was developing cracks.

Japanese imports and other competitors cut deeply into the TV bulb business, a product line that at one time accounted for half of Corning's revenues and three-quarters of its profits. By 1975, that business had become a money loser. Recession and lost profitability forced Corning through a series of recurring crises and retrenchments. Worldwide employment was cut by 37 percent. A major venture in integrated circuits was sold. Plants were sold or closed, and thousands of products were eliminated.

Through the late 1970s and early 1980s, a number of fortuitous developments pointed toward a new future for the venerable glassmaker. In each case, concepts developed in the company's laboratories had serendipitous consequences for future products and businesses. Work on safety windshields failed to produce results in that field but led to marketable breakthroughs involving liquid crystal displays. In another case, Corning pioneered the development of heat exchangers for gas turbine vehicles. Although the vehicles never materialized in significant numbers, the honeycomb substrates produced in the Corning labs could be used in the ceramic core of a new product: the catalytic converter. When air quality regulations required every automobile sold in the United States to use a catalytic converter, Corning's specialty materials business benefited.

Fiber optics was another field in which an unanticipated conjunction of events created a new and significant business for Corning. Super-thin glass fibers known as "light pipes" had been produced experimentally in the nineteenth century. These fibers have much greater capacity for carrying information (in the form of digital bits and bytes) than copper wires and transmit a clearer signal.

Corning began work on fiber optics in the mid-1960s, and continued working to improve the technology so that light-wave impulses could be transmitted over longer and longer distances. It developed this remarkable product and held all existing patents on its manufacture. Unfortunately, there were no buyers. "It was as if Corning had invented the carburetor in the 1850s," one observer remarked.[2] In the United States, AT&T still controlled the telephone market and estimated that it would continue using copper cables for the next 30 years. Foreign phone companies were equally unreceptive. By 1982, Corning had spent 17 years and $100 million on development of fiber optics but still had no serious customers. Then, as if to show that the gods smile on companies that don't give up easily, the AT&T empire was broken apart by court order, and new long-distance phone companies like MCI began to appear. With no fixed investments in copper cables, MCI saw an opportunity to leapfrog ahead of AT&T with the latest technology, and worked out a supplier contract with Corning. By 1986, Corning was selling $200 million worth of fiber optics. Revenues for this business had grown to just under $1 billion by 1994. Corning controlled half the world market, and was estimated to be the lowest cost producer in the industry.

Although the seeds of future growth had been planted, the rewards of fiber optics came too late to help Amory (Amo) Houghton, Jr., great-great-grandson of the founder who, in 1983, resigned and passed the keys to the glass empire to his younger brother, Jamie.

Writing of his brother, Jamie Houghton said, "chairman for 19 years, he was a fervent believer in technology. He single-handedly nurtured the fiber optic business through 17 years of losses because he believed, correctly, in the enormous potential of the business."

The younger Houghton stepped into command of a company

that was performing poorly and was bucking a recession in key markets. Nearly 70 percent of its revenues were coming from slow-growing businesses in which it held low to middling market shares. Profits had declined for three years in a row. Quality was not up to standards in many units.

From that low ebb Corning has emerged as one of the remarkable growth champions among large American corporations. To a large degree, that turnaround originated in a change of strategy and attitude initiated by its new management team.

To a major extent, the new strategy relied on the careful retention of Corning's key strengths. But the retention of some aspects of Corning was accompanied by revolutionary events in others. "Corning is not about glass," he wrote in the company's 1983 annual report, "it's about change." And he made plenty of changes. He and the company's management committee wasted little time before selling off marginal businesses—pharmaceutical tubing, electronics, biotechnology, and even its venerated light bulb business. Funds from these sales were directed toward acquisitions in laboratory services—a new field for the company—and alliances with other firms in varied areas.

Working through alliances is a long-standing Corning tradition. As early as 1920, the company had joined with the preeminent French glassmaker, St. Gobain, to introduce its Pyrex cookware to Europe. Corning formed other substantial alliances during the 1940s, creating companies such as Pittsburgh Corning, Dow Corning, and Owens-Corning Fiberglas. By 1968, its many allied ventures were contributing 20 percent of the company's profits, and 50 percent by 1993. Under the new regime, the number of these alliances multiplied. In October 1994, Houghton described the reasons behind the existence of three such arrangements:

- To gain access to markets the company could not otherwise penetrate—Samsung-Corning provided an opportunity to bring Corning television tube technology to the Asian market.
- To market technology developed by Corning—Dow Corning was formed to combine the expertise of the two participants in organic and inorganic materials in order to market silicone.

- To bring another firm's technology to a market where Corning is already established—Cormetech, an alliance of Corning and Mitsubishi, was formed to use the latter's coating technology to extend Corning's emissions control business.

Over the years, Corning has been involved with almost 50 alliances.

At the same time, Corning began a serious program of companywide quality improvement as a means of reducing costs and strengthening its product advantages, a program that extended to employees, customers, and suppliers. Payoffs were visible within just a few years. At MetPath, Corning's clinical lab testing units, 24-hour-or-faster delivery of test results jumped from 88 percent in 1986 to 98.5 percent in 1991. Customer returns of optical fiber dropped from 6,800 parts per million in 1986 to less than 1,000 in 1991. In its Cellular Ceramics plant, defects were reduced from 10,000 parts per million to 3 parts per million in just a few years.[3] Later, in 1991, serious work on process engineering (under the label "Corning Competes") was begun.

By the beginning of 1995, the Corning turnaround was paying off, and most observers were optimistic about the company's prospects. Results for 1994 suggested a strong return to profitability, with net income over $281 million on revenues surpassing $4.7 billion. The new Corning was oriented around four businesses linked by company values, technology, and shared resources: consumer housewares, specialty materials, telecommunications, and laboratory sciences. Not all businesses were prospering. Dow Corning, for example, suffered from health risks associated with silicone breast implants. But most of Corning's businesses were positioned for strong future growth and were expected to fuel the company's drive toward its announced goal of 12 percent annual earnings per share growth and an 18 percent return on equity.

Clearly, Corning's successful rebound from decline was accomplished because of improvements on a number of important fronts. In terms of our growth framework, we observe the following:

- New product development and strategic divestitures/acquisitions made it possible for the company to attack markets where its technologies could be brought to bear for higher levels of growth.

- Companywide quality initiatives and reengineering through "Corning Competes" boosted the company's value proposition and its ability to execute.
- Alliances improved the economics across the value chain of Corning's businesses.

Of these accomplishments, the last is worth looking at in detail.

Earlier chapters of this book described the importance of looking at the entire chain of activities that provide value to customers. Successful companies find opportunities to increase that value, and to capture the higher-value links of the chain. We also remarked on the importance of partnering with organizations that possess superior skills in certain areas of the value chain—skills that exceed those that your own firm can profitably provide.

Corning has shown remarkable dexterity in both of those approaches. As a manufacturer of laboratory glassware, Corning had been an important supplier to the hundreds of independent medical testing labs in the United States. That part of the value chain, unfortunately, was one of the *least* profitable; glassware had become a commodity-like business. The truly value-adding link in the chain was in the actual testing process.

Corning knew from its experience as a supplier to this industry that most independent testing labs were small, highly inefficient, and slow in providing test results to the doctors, hospitals, and health maintenance organizations they served. It recognized that growth and profits were available to any company that could reduce costs and provide higher service levels to customers. In 1982, the company created its laboratory services to address that opportunity through a number of strategic acquisitions, beginning with Met-Path, now a $1.3 billion operation that continues to grow as the health care industry's need for low-cost lab testing expands. The company's laboratory services also include Corning Pharmaceutical Services, which offers clinical research services to drug companies.

By 1993, laboratory services accounted for a third of Corning's revenues and 30 percent of its profits. Better still, these revenues and profits were both growing at double-digit rates. The truth of Jamie Houghton's remark that "Corning is not about glass, it's about change" was borne out in the transformation.

A similar exercise in value chain orchestration is demonstrated by Corning's extensive and generally successful use of business alliances. Recognizing its lack of market access, technology, or other requirements for dominance in one or another business, Corning has carefully chosen partners to improve the economics of the value chain in which it operates.

In the spring of 1995, Corning President and Chief Operating Officer Roger Ackerman commented on the company's future: "Corning has made a remarkable series of changes in order to grow and prosper for so long, but I believe that we will need to make even bigger changes and make them even faster in order to add the next chapters to the story."

BACK TO BASICS AND EXCELLENCE AT CABOT CORPORATION

The earlier discussion of Nucor and its success in making money "in an industry that doesn't do so well" should have made the point that growth can be found in virtually any sector of the economy. The case of Cabot Corporation underscores this point. After years of fruitless diversification, this venerable company returned to its traditional pursuit of making carbon black, the focus of its business for over a century.

It's hard to imagine a more unglamorous business than burning crude oil to produce carbon black, a very fine black powder used as a reinforcing agent in tires and most other rubber, as well as in inks, plastics, and coatings. As described by the *Wall Street Journal,* it is "a dreary business, beset by low innovation, rising environmental costs and skimpy profits."[4] This is exactly the type of business that every board and every CEO would want to move away from—which is just what Cabot's leadership did during the 1980s, when the strategy of diversifying into entirely new ventures was still widely touted by consultants as an elixir for growth.

For Cabot, carbon black was the cash cow used to finance ventures into specialized crystals, semiconductors, ceramics, oil and gas, and other businesses in which it had neither technical nor managerial expertise. Unfortunately, the profits sought through these ventures failed to pan out, and most of Cabot's investments evaporated. By 1985, the company was experiencing such financial distress that it began downsizing its operations, selling 40 percent of its assets.[5]

In most cases, we'd expect a company like this to play by the script and gradually slide into industrial oblivion. But the Cabot story is shaping up toward a different ending, one that should encourage executives in every old-line industry.

Cabot returned to its traditional carbon black business, but it did so with renewed energy and commitment on several fronts. On the production side, management sought newly created operating efficiencies and established production in the growing markets of Asia. Under the direction of its new chairman, Sam Bodman, significant investments were made in modern facilities, technology, and training. On the product side, the company spent $205 million on R&D between 1990 and 1995, developing special proprietary materials with high-value applications: carbon black and titanium dioxide concentrates for use in plastic compounds and a carbon black designed to reduce the rolling resistance of automobile tires. The first results of these valued-added products began to be seen in 1994 and 1995.

While the turnaround of Cabot Corporation is not complete, the company has taken the steps necessary to survive and has positioned itself for future growth. By focusing on the development of high-value new products and production efficiencies, it has improved both the value proposition it offers its customers and the economics of the manufacturer while staying with the business it knows best.

A TIMELY INTERVENTION AT HEWLETT-PACKARD

As we were completing this book early in 1995, it was difficult to imagine Hewlett-Packard sliding toward the same abyss of problems that have afflicted so many once-great companies over the years. Today, Hewlett-Packard's reputation for quality and reliability, its capacity for inventiveness, and its strong record of profitable growth would seem an impenetrable armor against the ills that afflict many companies. The picture in 1990, however, was far less rosy. Profits had dropped like a rock. Major development projects languished. Many employees were frustrated and demoralized. Hewlett-Packard stood at a fork in the road. How it proceeded would determine its organizational vitality for years to come.

In the absence of action, Hewlett-Packard would have joined some of its earlier peers among the fallen angels. But intervention by the company's traditional leaders guided Hewlett-Packard onto another course, and that, as the poet said, has made all the difference.

Hewlett-Packard's problem in 1990 was creeping centralization, a common side effect of past success. The decade of the 1980s had been a prosperous one for Hewlett-Packard. Sales had grown from $3.1 billion to $11.9 billion. Market value had increased by a factor of 12. But prosperity and growth had begun to divert Hewlett-Packard from its tradition of autonomous divisions into a company controlled from the center. During the mid- to late 1980s, central R&D and marketing took control of functions once scattered throughout the divisions. Project managers who once made decisions for their own units now had to obtain approvals from several committees. Pricing and payment policies were determined by corporate staffers.

The effects of creeping centralization were very soon apparent. Important efforts to break into personal computer and workstation markets languished. Development projects were slow to take focus and slower to move to market. High costs jeopardized the competitiveness of newly introduced products. Profits in 1990 and 1991 slumped.

Centralization was alien to HP tradition. Founders Bill Hewlett and David Packard had followed the principle of splitting up any division that grew too big, giving each unit responsibility for its own engineering, marketing, and production. Whenever a division grew beyond 1,500 employees, Hewlett and Packard would break it apart.[6] Many attribute the company's greatest successes in palm-sized computers, workstations, and laser printers to the great independence given its separate businesses. Unlike Digital, there was no single voice to give direction. And unlike IBM, there was no company line. Instead, HP was a confederation of highly entrepreneurial operations.

The shift from autonomy to centralization may have been the result of a major initiative, begun in 1983, to develop a RISC chip workstation named Spectrum. Spectrum was a huge financial gamble for the company, and central control of its development seemed, at the time, the best way to deal with it. "We grew up with a decentralized organization," then CEO John Young said later. "For Spectrum, we needed to bring in people from different parts of the company. We wound up with an organization that didn't work."[7]

Fortunately, reform was swift and effective. In October 1990, Hewlett and Packard, as major shareholders and company icons, stepped in to nip the problem in the bud. Working with CEO Young, the two octogenarians took a number of dramatic steps to return the company to its decentralized tradition. Dozens of committees were dissolved, two layers of management were eliminated, and product groups were given their own sales staffs. Results were not slow in coming. By 1992, time to market for new products was cut roughly in half, the number of product launches doubled, and profits were back on track. The ability to act decisively made it possible for the company's languishing PC division to engineer its own turnaround. By 1995 it had turned from being a nonentity in this highly competitive market to become the second-fastest grower.[8]

This tale underscores the importance of one of our growth foundations: organizational alignment. The strategy of Hewlett-Packard did not change all through this period; developing new high-tech products for a broad range of markets continued to animate the company. Unfortunately, that strategy had been undermined by the move toward centralized control.

The customers and markets served by the many Hewlett-Packard divisions were too varied and fast-changing for a centralized organization to serve effectively. Centralized control of product development, pricing policies, and sales failed to support the strategy that had made Hewlett-Packard great. Once the organization was properly aligned—with decision-making power returned to the operating units—the company snapped back to its winning ways. Business performance during the years following that realignment was among the best that Hewlett-Packard had ever experienced.

A WAKE-UP CALL FOR UPS

United Parcel Service is another accomplished company that came very close to losing its edge, yet responded in an effective way. As the dominant player in the fast-growing, fast-changing field of package and document delivery, it was hit simultaneously by waves of new competition and technological change. As in the previous cases, decisive leadership and skillful management of change saved it from becoming just another formerly great company.

Since its founding in 1907, United Parcel Service of America, Inc. (UPS) has become the nation's largest package deliverer. Today, it serves more than 200 countries with 130,000 delivery vehicles and one of the world's largest fleets of aircraft. It makes some 11.5 million daily deliveries, using an advanced system of communications and computers.

In the decades prior to 1980, UPS had only one serious rival— the U.S. Postal Service—and it grew and profited by being everything that the Postal Service was not: efficient, fast, and dependable. Like the AT&T-Bell nationwide phone system before its enforced breakup in the 1980s, UPS was driven by the urge to improve internal efficiency and lower costs, even in the absence of competitive pressures. Its logistics experts worked out optimal routines for picking up and moving packages around and between American cities. Its brown-uniformed drivers followed regular "loop" routes designed to increase UPS efficiency.

To a great extent, UPS created the rules and the pricing schedule. Business customers were assigned pickup and delivery times based on driver schedules. Pricing followed a no-discount formula based on weight and geographic zones that applied equally to customers large and small. A mother sending cookies to her children at summer camp enjoyed the same rates as the corporate customer shipping thousands of packages each month.

This was a classic "company-driven" system. UPS defined the terms and customers received the benefits of its legendary efficiency.

From an organizational point of view, UPS had engineered the perfect blueprint for moving packages. From top to bottom, the components of the blueprint fit together with precision. Everyone understood the routines for picking up and delivering packages; virtually every manager in the company started at the bottom of the ladder and worked each step toward the top. Incentives were aligned with the company's mission. Efficiency was a corporate virtue. UPS had one price, one daily pickup and delivery, one way for customers to use its service.

This system worked just fine for UPS as long as its key competitor was the U.S. Postal Service. During the 1980s, however, this situation changed. Federal Express—already a player in the air delivery market—had been dismissed as simply a letter carrier with small airplanes. But eventually this challenger had to be taken seriously. Its next-day service provided something UPS could not. More important, its ability to provide real-time tracking and tracing of every package made it possible for Federal Express to guarantee delivery schedules and to charge tremendous premiums. To the amazement of UPS managers, customers were willing to pay more than twice UPS's rates for the benefits of overnight service and the ability to track their packages en route.

New competition from Roadway Package System (RPS), however, was impossible to ignore. Its entry into the business sent shudders through the ranks of UPS. Roadway was not a bit player, but a new subsidiary of a major freight handler with a nationwide infrastructure of offices and trucks. Worse, it struck directly at the heart of UPS's business—the large-scale shipper. Unlike its established rival, RPS scheduled service based on customer needs, not on the needs of its system. More threatening still, it identified the most profitable segments of the market and used price breaks to take them away from UPS. Initially, UPS managers were stunned and even puzzled by these losses.

Though an expanding market for package delivery and international expansion kept UPS's revenues on an upward trajectory dur-

ing the late 1980s, these new and more flexible competitors damp-
ened the company's growth and profits. Clearly, UPS had to
change if it hoped to avoid becoming a corporate "shrinker" in the
years ahead.

The job of leading the response to these challengers fell to UPS
chief executive Kent "Oz" Nelson. Like other senior managers of
the company, Nelson was a lifelong employee. But unlike his predecessors at the top of this operations-driven organization, his
experience had been almost entirely in sales, customer service, and
marketing. Working through his management team and employees
down to the delivery level, Nelson uncovered the dimensions of the
challenge and the need to retool services based on customer needs.

"We spent a good five months figuring out *how* to compete," he
told an interviewer from *Industry Week*. "We found out it was
harder than we thought it would be. All of a sudden, we had rivals
that were starting to take away segments of our business. But we
decided to take each one of them head on. We didn't want to walk
away from much. We wanted to compete! So we had to build new
competencies and offer new services."[9]

The cost of building those competencies would make any executive shudder: investing billions in information technology, adding
almost 4,000 employees in information services, scrapping the
time-honored rate card, creating many new services, and rethink-
ing the entire UPS system for optimizing cost and efficiency.

Nelson recognized that technology would be a fundamental tool
for providing greater customer service *and* improved operating
efficiencies. Starting in 1986 with a rudimentary information system, he and Information Services Vice President Frank Erbrick set
out to build a system capable of tracking every UPS package. Six
years and more than $2 billion later, the company had the best
tracking system in the industry. In the years since, it has developed
a mobile wireless data system using 70 cellular phone carriers to
transmit information from each of its thousands of delivery vehicles. Today, UPS drivers record all pickup and delivery information—even personal signatures—into a hand-held computer. The
information is downloaded through cellular transmission channels

to the UPS database, eliminating time, paperwork, and costly errors. The electronic signature system alone has reduced recording errors from one in 100 deliveries to less than one in 300.[10]

By 1994, UPS had successfully developed both the customer-oriented services needed to retain competitive superiority and the technological capabilities needed to maintain its tradition of low-cost, reliable package delivery. Together, these helped the company earn more than $900 million in profits on almost $20 billion in sales.

In terms of the growth framework developed in this book, Nelson and his company reinvented UPS in a way that made use of all of our growth strategies and the foundations that support them.

Strategy

On the strategy front, UPS dropped its tradition of treating customers as an undifferentiated mass. Taking a cue from Roadway, it began segmenting its market, offering price discounts to attract and hold high-value customers. It developed new products, such as next-day air and international service. It even found new channels for connecting its services with customers: drop boxes in convenient locations and partnerships with package service centers such as Mail Boxes Etc.

Value

For the first time in its long history, UPS let the customer dictate its services. This meant new products and pickup and delivery times that matched customer needs, and package tracking capabilities that increased the value of UPS service to its customers.

Economics

Reinvention of the UPS system in terms that suited customers threatened to blow a hole in the company's time-tested blueprint for efficient, low-cost service. But logistics engineering was a company strength, and it quickly found ways to deliver new, higher-level services with remarkable efficiency. The technology described earlier was a large part of the solution. And the alliance it formed with 70 cellular phone companies brought to the value chain capabilities that UPS on its own was clearly unable to fill.

To the surprise of management, the redesign effort led to a number of money-saving discoveries. Next-day service, for example, required new sorting procedures that led to more uniform and cost-effective work flows. As Nelson said later, "We wound up saving ourselves money while giving faster service."[11]

Execution

Effective execution is what UPS has always been about. Work activities and incentives were realigned so that the organization truly served the company's new business strategy. Counting all its deliveries and sorting of packages, UPS has 23 million opportunities to execute well or poorly every day. It trained personnel to make its new system work exceedingly well—both for customers and for its own bottom line.

The makeover of UPS contains important lessons for any executive determined to return his or her company to profitable growth. Patience is one; a willingness to make the necessary investments is another. Nelson and his managers spent five months just getting a handle on their competitive problems. Implementation of the technology plan alone took a full five years and $2 billion, with continuing improvements and investments thereafter.

Other lessons were spelled out by Nelson himself in *Industry Week:*[12]

- "Don't be afraid to ask employees to embrace new ideas when business conditions change, because employees will—maybe faster than you think."
- "Don't be afraid to rethink your business, because your competitors already are."
- "Don't forget to sweat the details, because that's what business is."
- "Don't forget to train front-line employees, because they're the ones who delight—or displease—your customers."

The four turnaround stories just examined indicate how corporate growth can be rekindled. At least two issues remain, however. The first is whether every company should immediately set out on a path to growth. The second involves the methods by which transformational leaders redirect a business from a situation in which it does not meet the standards posed by our growth framework to one in which it does.

In Chapter 7 we argued that there is no universally correct organizational structure. We should extend that and also state that there is no universally correct corporate strategy. Even growth, which we greatly favor, can be the wrong goal for some business leaders. In May 1994, we met with a demanding panel of corporate leaders to "test market" our thoughts on growth. This group gave us a list of circumstances under which growth is an inappropriate goal:

- *When the business needs to shrink first.* One executive pointed out that "growing a mess simply creates a larger mess." The "mess" must be eliminated first, and that is sometimes best accomplished through a thoughtful program of restructuring or process reengineering. The important thing to remember is that shrinking is a *means* to returning to growth, not an end in itself.

- *When survival is the issue.* Growth can be a dangerous distraction for a business that is fighting for its life. When a lifeboat is sinking, the crew has to lighten the load or risk losing everyone. This involves difficult and morally painful choices. Business survival also involves painful choices about who and what will stay, and who and what must go over the side if the organization is to stay afloat. We have seen situations in which the best people and much of the company's money were tied up in long-term growth initiatives, even though cash conservation and every ounce of corporate energy were required to stay alive in the short term.

- *When the owners would be better off without growth.* Many readers of this book will be involved with small or medium-sized family businesses. For them, growth may be inappropriate if the result is a company too large for the family to own and/or manage.

- *When growth creates financial stress or loss of control.* Growth must be funded from internal or external sources. In cases where cash flows cannot meet the financing requirements of growth, capital must be borrowed from banks or bondholders. Both increase financial risk and may involve operating restrictions. For small and medium-sized companies, new equity capital usually results in a loss of control for the original shareholders and managers. In some cases, financing may simply be unavailable.

Our second question concerns the methods of transformational leadership. None of our turnaround examples "just happened" or bubbled up from the bottom of the organization. Bodman at Cabot, the founders at Hewlett-Packard, the Houghton family at Corning, and Nelson at UPS all had to move mountains to restart growth. They had to explain, lead, inspire, and stay in front. The art of transformational leadership has been the subject of entire books and we cannot hope to adequately address it here. We have observed, however, some common factors in successful turnarounds:

- *Establish the business case.* No organization takes drastic action in response to minor irritation. In the successful turnarounds we have seen, the motivation for change was compelling and crystal clear to the entire organization. For many companies, a "near-death experience" is what makes them ready for and accepting of change.
- *Address the real problems.* Attempted turnarounds fail when executives attack symptoms instead of the real disease. The honesty required to acknowledge all the sources of the problem can be overwhelming.
- *Communicate, communicate, communicate.* Every employee who must change his or her behavior for change to succeed must be thoroughly informed of the reasons. All too often, a 30-minute video tries to justify changes that the management team has argued about for months. The video is a good start, but the need for explanation, inspiration, and training is often grossly underestimated.
- *Never expect a stable future.* Indiana Jones was attacked by a succession of villains. Some turnarounds achieve initial success and then relax as a false sense of security grows. The most important single thing for an organization to learn is that *change must be permanent.*

- *Avoid misalignment in the new strategy.* It does no good to point the organization in one direction if compensation beckons employees in other directions. The many factors identified in Chapter 7 as creating alignment or misalignment in the organization must all be brought together in a relatively short time.
- *Consider the need for reinvention.* Some of the most tragic tales of corporate disappearance involve companies that needed to do more than tinker with improvement. Railway Express was once the preeminent small-package shipper. If management had been open to reinvention, the company could be doing today what UPS and Federal Express are doing. Nothing but inertia and institutional loyalty prevented the firm from reinventing its value chain to incorporate new shipping technologies.

Our continuing study of growth is alternately inspiring and daunting. Inspiring because profitable growth is possible in any company in any industry; because the people we meet in profitable growth companies are happy to be there; and because there are no mysterious secrets to growth. Daunting because the odds are so long and the work of growth is so hard and unrelenting. On balance, however, we believe that the case for hope is more convincing than the case for fear. The leaders of profitable growth companies create prosperity and personal satisfaction for themselves and for thousands of employees.

You can do likewise.

Appendix A

GROWTH DIAGNOSTIC

"DIAGNOSING" YOUR COMPANY'S
GROWTH PROBLEMS

✳

We realize that we may have presented almost too much helpful advice in this book. No company can do everything and no company can do too much at once. Where should you begin? What matters most?

We have encapsulated the logic flow of our advice in the attached flow chart. If you have the necessary information required to answer the questions posed by the flow chart, you can ask them and follow the chart to more questions until you eventually reach a general recommendation concerning the types of business action that may do the most to help your company grow.

Simplistic and written without specific knowledge of your business, the chart will obviously need to be viewed with some caution. We have tried the logic flow, however, on some businesses we know well, and the results come close, very close, to the output of more sophisticated analysis. At a minimum, the questions asked, the order in which they occur, and the general nature of the recommendations may serve the reader as a helpful "skeleton" in designing a more specific course of inquiry for asking the question, "How can I make this business grow?"

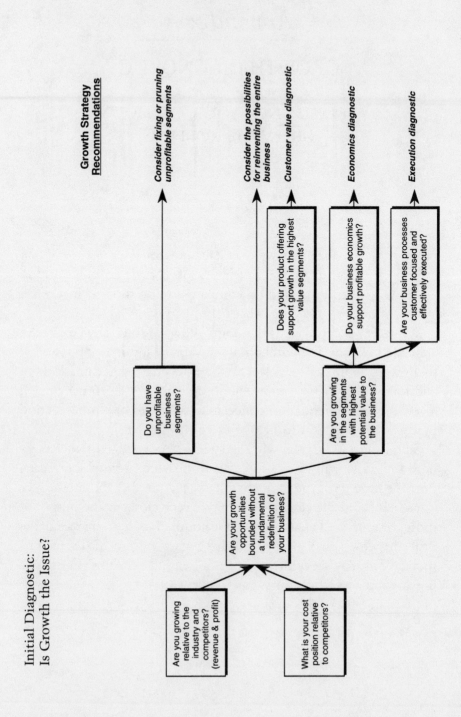

Initial Diagnostic:
Is Growth the Issue?

Growth Strategy Recommendations

Consider fixing or pruning unprofitable segments

Consider the possibilities for reinventing the entire business

Customer value diagnostic

Economics diagnostic

Execution diagnostic

Do you have unprofitable business segments?

Does your product offering support growth in the highest value segments?

Do your business economics support profitable growth?

Are your business processes customer focused and effectively executed?

Are your growth opportunities bounded without a fundamental redefinition of your business?

Are you growing in the segments with highest potential value to the business?

Are you growing relative to the industry and competitors? (revenue & profit)

What is your cost position relative to competitors?

Customer Value Diagnostic:
Does Your Product Line Support Growth?

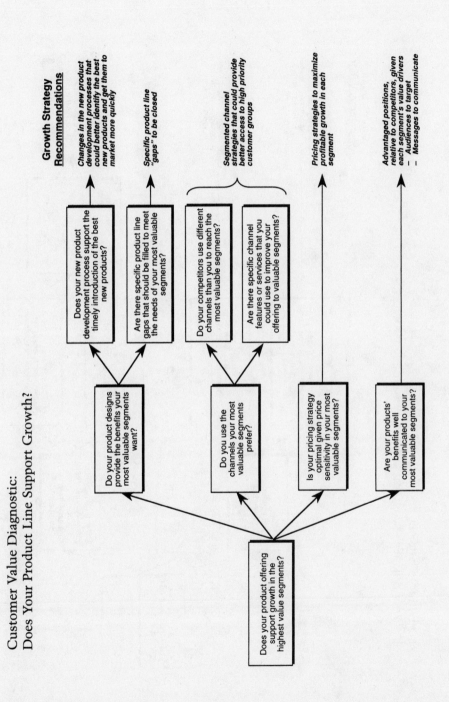

Economics Diagnostic:
Do Your Business Economics Support Profitable Growth?

**Growth Strategy
Recommendations**

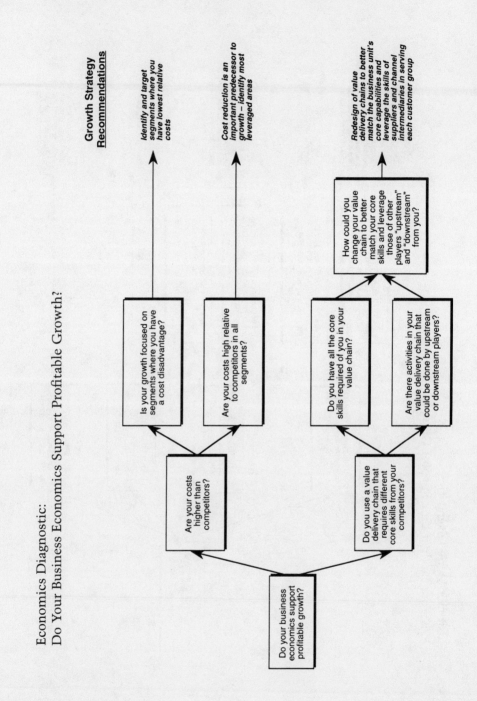

*Identify and target
segments where you
have lowest relative
costs*

*Cost reduction is an
important predecessor to
growth – identify most
leveraged areas*

*Redesign of value
delivery chains to better
match the business unit's
core capabilities and
leverage the skills of
suppliers and channel
intermediaries in serving
each customer group*

Is your growth focused on
segments where you have
a cost disadvantage?

Are your costs high relative
to competitors in all
segments?

How could you
change your value
chain to better
match your core
skills and leverage
those of other
players "upstream"
and "downstream"
from you?

Are your costs
higher than
competitors?

Do you have all the core
skills required of you in your
value chain?

Are there activities in your
value delivery chain that
could be done by upstream
or downstream players?

Do you use a value
delivery chain that
requires different
core skills from your
competitors?

Do your business
economics support
profitable growth?

Execution Diagnostic:
Does Your Process Execution Support Growth?

**Growth Strategy
Recommendations**

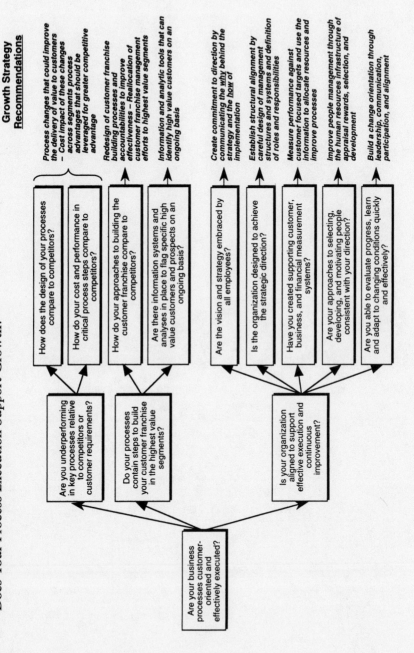

*Process changes that could improve
the delivery of value to customers
– Cost impact of these changes
across segments process
advantages that should be
leveraged for greater competitive
advantage*

*Redesign of customer franchise
building processes and
accountabilities to improve
effectiveness – Reallocation of
customer franchise management
efforts to highest value segments*

*Information and analytic tools that can
identify high value customers on an
ongoing basis*

*Create commitment to direction by
communicating the why behind the
strategy and the how of
implementation*

*Establish structural alignment by
careful design of management
structures and systems and definition
of roles and responsibilities*

*Measure performance against
customer focused targets and use the
information to allocate resources and
improve processes*

*Improve people management through
the human resources infrastructure of
appraisal rewards, selection, and
development*

*Build a change orientation through
leadership, communication,
participation, and alignment*

How does the design of your processes
compare to competitors?

How do your cost and performance in
critical process steps compare to
competitors?

How do your approaches to building the
customer franchise compare to
competitors?

Are there information systems and
analyses in place to flag specific high
value customers and prospects on an
ongoing basis?

Are the vision and strategy embraced by
all employees?

Is the organization designed to achieve
the strategic direction?

Have you created supporting customer,
business, and financial measurement
systems?

Are your approaches to selecting,
developing, and motivating people
consistent with your direction?

Are you able to evaluate progress, learn
and adapt to changing conditions quickly
and effectively?

Are you underperforming
in key processes relative
to competitors or
customer requirements?

Do your processes
contain steps to build
your customer franchise
in the highest value
segments?

Is your organization
aligned to support
effective execution and
continuous
improvement?

Are your business
processes customer-
oriented and
effectively executed?

Appendix B

A LIST OF "GROWTH CHAMPIONS"

✳

W e have referred throughout the book to our analysis of large U.S. public corporations. Many of our conclusions on the value of growth were based on this work and most, but not all, of our understanding of growth strategies was drawn from further examination of the "profitable growers" within this sample.

The companies listed in this appendix are profitable growers—those which outperformed their industry groups (using industry definitions as developed by *Fortune* magazine) in both revenue growth and operating profit growth for the period from 1988 to 1993.

Profitable Growers

Company Name	Fortune Industry	Company Size Revenue 93 (000s)	88-93 Company Revenue Growth	88-93 Company Operating Profit Growth	88-93 Industry Revenue Growth	88-93 Industry Operating Profit Growth
3com Corp.	Electronics and Electrical Equipment	$617,168	19.62%	9.68%	5.09%	9.16%
A.O. Smith Corp.	Motor Vehicles and Parts	$1,193,900	3.29%	13.99%	2.73%	-4.44%
Abbott Laboratories	Pharmaceuticals	$8,407,800	11.24%	11.79%	10.18%	3.55%
Advanced Micro Devices Inc.	Electronics and Electrical Equipment	$1,648,300	7.92%	84.73%	5.09%	9.16%
Advanta Corp.	Diversified Financial	$406,961	15.67%	67.86%	2.73%	7.24%
Air Products and Chemicals Inc.	Chemicals	$3,327,700	6.47%	4.91%	-0.40%	-8.42%
Airborne Freight Corp.	Transportation	$1,720,000	17.50%	30.02%	7.64%	0.69%
Albertsons Inc.	Retailing	$11,283,700	10.75%	19.29%	7.22%	5.59%
Alco Health Services Corp.	Diversified Services	$3,719,000	12.56%	9.42%	7.95%	0.19%
Alco Standard Corp.	Diversified Services	$6,591,300	11.59%	7.78%	7.95%	0.19%
Alleghany Corp.	Diversified Financial	$1,908,500	17.11%	126.23%	2.73%	7.24%
Alltel Corp.	Diversified Services	$2,342,087	17.00%	15.73%	7.95%	0.19%
America West Airlines Inc.	Transportation	$1,325,400	11.31%	46.17%	7.64%	0.69%
American Family Life Assurance Co.	Life Insurance	$4,923,100	17.19%	16.04%	7.03%	7.02%
American Greetings Corp.	Publishing and Printing	$1,780,815	7.29%	21.99%	3.51%	0.48%
American International Group Inc.	Diversified Financial	$20,134,700	8.85%	13.54%	2.73%	7.24%
American Standard Inc.	Building Materials and Glass	$3,830,500	8.93%	6.36%	1.88%	-4.69%
Amgen Inc.	Pharmaceuticals	$1,373,800	81.27%	253.53%	10.18%	3.55%
Amsouth Bancorporation	Commercial Banking	$656,438	12.23%	16.27%	10.69%	15.00%
Amsted Industries Inc.	Metals	$868,130	1.08%	-2.84%	-1.18%	-29.36%
Anacomp Inc.	Scientific, Photographic, Control Equipment	$590,208	5.55%	4.06%	4.24%	2.91%
Anchor Glass Container Corp.	Building Materials and Glass	$1,126,000	2.86%	-1.51%	1.88%	-4.69%
Aon Corp.	Diversified Financial	$3,844,800	7.07%	13.48%	2.73%	7.24%
Apple Computer Inc.	Computers and Office Equipment	$7,977,000	14.40%	-7.02%	6.22%	-14.08%
Applied Materials Inc.	Industrial and Farm Equipment	$1,080,000	24.38%	18.37%	4.51%	7.25%
Arkansas Best Corp.	Transportation	$1,009,900	23.83%	11.76%	7.64%	0.69%
Arrow Electronics Inc.	Diversified Services	$2,535,600	20.30%	38.75%	7.95%	0.19%
Arvin Industries Inc.	Motor Vehicles and Parts	$1,939,400	8.11%	8.05%	2.73%	-4.44%
AST Research Inc.	Computers and Office Equipment	$1,412,200	27.89%	21.33%	6.22%	-14.08%
AT&T Corp.	Telecommunications	$67,156,000	13.78%	124.90%	7.59%	11.38%

186

Profitable Growers (continued)

Company Name	Fortune Industry	Company Size Revenue 93 (000s)	88-93 Company Revenue Growth	88-93 Company Operating Profit Growth	88-93 Industry Revenue Growth	88-93 Industry Operating Profit Growth
Automatic Data Processing Inc.	Computers and Office Equipment	$2,223,400	7.49%	8.35%	6.22%	-14.08%
Avery Dennison Corp.	Forest and Paper Products	$2,608,700	10.52%	2.95%	3.87%	-10.32%
Baltimore Gas and Electric Co.	Utilities	$2,668,700	7.45%	4.56%	3.89%	3.98%
Banc One Corp.	Commercial Banking	$5,581,742	29.65%	31.17%	10.69%	15.00%
Bancorp Hawaii Inc.	Commercial Banking	$602,697	14.63%	22.60%	10.69%	15.00%
The Bank of New York Co. Inc.	Commercial Banking	$2,816,000	17.20%	24.33%	10.69%	15.00%
Bankamerica Corp.	Commercial Banking	$11,714,000	16.59%	32.51%	10.69%	15.00%
Banponce Corp.	Commercial Banking	$617,308	35.23%	41.74%	10.69%	15.00%
Banta Corp.	Publishing and Printing	$698,000	5.79%	11.34%	3.51%	0.48%
Barnett Banks Inc.	Commercial Banking	$2,249,843	11.05%	15.59%	10.69%	15.00%
Baroid Corp.	Chemicals	$846,164	11.45%	77.55%	-0.40%	-8.42%
Bausch and Lomb	Scientific, Photographic, Control Equipment	$1,872,200	13.86%	10.08%	4.24%	2.91%
Baxter International Inc.	Scientific, Photographic, Control Equipment	$8,879,000	5.29%	8.24%	4.24%	2.91%
Bay View Capital Corp.	Savings Institutions	$80,151	7.97%	-4.91%	5.28%	-7.26%
BB&T Financial Corp.	Commercial Banking	$440,252	18.68%	26.20%	10.69%	15.00%
Bear, Stearns and Cos. Inc.	Diversified Financial	$2,856,900	8.57%	26.02%	2.73%	7.24%
Becton, Dickinson and Co.	Scientific, Photographic, Control Equipment	$2,465,400	7.60%	4.46%	4.24%	2.91%
Beneficial Corp.	Diversified Financial	$1,957,500	6.66%	13.42%	2.73%	7.24%
Bergen Brunswig Corp.	Diversified Services	$6,823,600	14.37%	8.11%	7.95%	0.19%
Berkshire Hathaway Inc.	Apparel	$3,653,483	9.38%	21.05%	9.09%	12.56%
Betz Laboratories Inc.	Chemicals	$684,900	8.88%	9.11%	-0.40%	-8.42%
Bindley Western Industries Inc.	Diversified Services	$3,426,100	21.86%	18.20%	7.95%	0.19%
Black and Decker Corp.	Industrial and Farm Equipment	$4,882,200	16.44%	15.64%	4.51%	7.25%
Boatmens Bancshares Inc.	Commercial Banking	$1,474,831	17.19%	42.92%	10.69%	15.00%
The Boeing Co.	Aerospace	$25,285,000	8.31%	30.43%	2.85%	6.21%
The Boston Bancorp	Savings Institutions	$91,056	15.55%	16.18%	5.28%	-7.26%
Briggs and Stratton Corp.	Industrial and Farm Equipment	$1,139,500	4.51%	24.47%	4.51%	7.25%
Bristol-Myers Squibb Co.	Pharmaceuticals	$11,413,000	13.83%	9.97%	10.18%	3.55%
Browning-Ferris Industries Inc.	Diversified Services	$3,494,900	11.07%	1.29%	7.95%	0.19%
Capital Holding Corp.	Diversified Financial	$2,884,200	7.11%	13.43%	2.73%	7.24%

Profitable Growers (continued)

Company Name	Fortune Industry	Company Size Revenue 93 (000s)	88-93 Company Revenue Growth	88-93 Company Operating Profit Growth	88-93 Industry Revenue Growth	88-93 Industry Operating Profit Growth
Carnival Corp.	Transportation	$1,556,919	21.02%	17.07%	7.64%	0.69%
Carolina Power and Light Co.	Utilities	$2,895,400	4.96%	5.71%	3.89%	3.98%
Carpenter Technology Corp.	Metals	$576,248	0.73%	-2.78%	-1.18%	-29.36%
Centerior Energy Corp.	Utilities	$2,474,200	3.96%	19.25%	3.89%	3.98%
Centex Corp.	Diversified Services	$3,214,482	11.74%	22.90%	7.95%	0.19%
Central Fidelity Banks Inc.	Commercial Banking	$450,058	15.75%	19.96%	10.69%	15.00%
The Charles Schwab Corp.	Diversified Financial	$965,000	19.73%	73.14%	2.73%	7.24%
Charter One Financial Inc.	Savings Institutions	$196,480	32.83%	42.24%	5.28%	-7.26%
Chemical Banking Corp.	Commercial Banking	$8,660,000	18.95%	20.68%	10.69%	15.00%
Chevron Corp.	Petroleum Refining	$32,123,000	2.99%	-4.99%	2.04%	-7.74%
Chrysler Corp.	Motor Vehicles and Parts	$43,600,000	4.21%	3.66%	2.73%	-4.44%
Cincinnati Financial Corp.	Diversified Financial	$1,442,200	9.66%	11.75%	2.73%	7.24%
Cincinnati Gas and Electric Co.	Utilities	$1,751,741	4.80%	5.42%	3.89%	3.98%
Circuit City Stores Inc.	Retailing	$4,130,415	19.13%	11.71%	7.22%	5.59%
Cisco Systems Inc.	Electronics and Electrical Equipment	$649,035	159.65%	245.16%	5.09%	9.16%
Clark Refining and Marketing Inc.	Petroleum Refining	$2,252,964	66.59%	1.94%	2.04%	-7.74%
The Coastal Corp.	Petroleum Refining	$10,136,100	4.36%	-2.60%	2.04%	-7.74%
Coca Cola Bottling Co. Consolidated	Beverages	$687,000	15.92%	16.95%	8.90%	12.23%
The Coca Cola Co.	Beverages	$13,957,000	10.85%	14.18%	8.90%	12.23%
Collective Bancorp Inc.	Savings Institutions	$125,278	20.35%	28.84%	5.28%	-7.26%
Columbia First Bank, FSB	Savings Institutions	$69,553	9.34%	14.40%	5.28%	-7.26%
Comdisco Inc.	Diversified Services	$2,153,000	10.46%	2.21%	7.95%	0.19%
Comerica Inc.	Commercial Banking	$1,596,040	25.31%	27.57%	10.69%	15.00%
Compaq Computer Corp.	Computers and Office Equipment	$7,191,000	28.34%	10.92%	6.22%	-14.08%
Compass Bancshares Inc.	Commercial Banking	$427,474	18.10%	22.50%	10.69%	15.00%
Computer Associates International Inc.	Computers and Office Equipment	$1,841,000	12.31%	12.48%	6.22%	-14.08%
Computer Sciences Corp.	Computers and Office Equipment	$2,582,670	14.64%	12.74%	6.22%	-14.08%
Conagra Inc.	Food	$21,519,100	13.67%	22.00%	7.38%	9.42%
Cone Mills Corp.	Textiles	$769,200	2.26%	167.19%	-1.34%	3.62%
Connecticut General Life Insurance Inc.	Life Insurance	$8,521,700	11.82%	16.94%	7.03%	7.02%

Profitable Growers (continued)

Company Name	Fortune Industry	Company Size Revenue 93 (000s)	88-93 Company Revenue Growth	88-93 Company Operating Profit Growth	88-93 Industry Revenue Growth	88-93 Industry Operating Profit Growth
Consolidated Edison Co. of New York Inc.	Utilities	$6,265,400	4.17%	4.35%	3.89%	3.98%
Consolidated Natural Gas Co.	Utilities	$3,184,100	5.23%	4.08%	3.89%	3.98%
Cooper Tire and Rubber Co.	Rubber and Plastic Products	$1,193,600	9.80%	20.05%	3.61%	7.04%
Corestates Financial Corp.	Commercial Banking	$1,620,956	11.93%	15.59%	10.69%	15.00%
Corning Inc.	Building Materials and Glass	$4,004,800	13.55%	19.41%	1.88%	-4.69%
Costco Wholesale Corp.	Retailing	$7,649,400	30.39%	6.96%	7.22%	5.59%
CPC International Inc.	Food	$6,738,000	7.47%	9.53%	7.38%	9.42%
Crown Cork and Seal Co. Inc.	Metal Products	$4,162,600	17.81%	18.82%	7.06%	6.87%
CSF Holdings	Savings Institutions	$145,656	16.51%	40.87%	5.28%	-7.26%
Cummins Engine Co. Inc.	Industrial and Farm Equipment	$4,247,900	5.12%	32.68%	4.51%	7.25%
Dayton Hudson Corp.	Retailing	$19,233,000	9.52%	8.82%	7.22%	5.59%
Deere and Co.	Industrial and Farm Equipment	$7,693,800	7.48%	34.52%	4.51%	7.25%
The Dexter Corp.	Chemicals	$887,100	1.16%	-3.15%	-0.40%	-8.42%
Diamond Shamrock Inc.	Petroleum Refining	$2,555,300	7.21%	-4.21%	2.04%	-7.74%
Dibrell Brothers Inc.	Tobacco	$1,065,400	9.22%	19.76%	-2.42%	2.23%
Diebold Inc.	Computers and Office Equipment	$623,277	6.70%	13.56%	6.22%	-14.08%
Dillard Department Stores Inc.	Retailing	$5,130,600	14.08%	6.58%	7.22%	5.59%
Dow Corning Corp.	Chemicals	$2,043,700	6.71%	0.59%	-0.40%	-8.42%
Dr. Pepper/Seven-Up Companies Inc.	Beverages	$707,400	17.88%	26.11%	8.90%	12.23%
DSC Communications Corp.	Electronics and Electrical Equipment	$730,774	16.56%	29.47%	5.09%	9.16%
Duracell International Inc.	Electronics and Electrical Equipment	$1,742,200	6.88%	19.50%	5.09%	9.16%
E I Du Pont De Nemours and Co.	Chemicals	$32,621,000	-0.18%	-7.07%	-0.40%	-8.42%
Eaton Corp.	Motor Vehicles and Parts	$4,401,000	4.88%	-1.46%	2.73%	-4.44%
Echlin Inc.	Motor Vehicles and Parts	$1,944,500	8.48%	8.83%	2.73%	-4.44%
EG&G Inc.	Scientific, Photographic, Control Equipment	$2,697,900	13.92%	4.28%	4.24%	2.91%
EMC Corp.	Computers and Office Equipment	$782,621	44.72%	179.27%	6.22%	-14.08%
Entergy Corp.	Utilities	$4,485,300	4.70%	10.88%	3.89%	3.98%
Essex Group Inc.	Metals	$868,846	2.06%	-7.11%	-1.18%	-29.36%
Exxon Corp.	Petroleum Refining	$97,825,000	2.31%	-2.49%	2.04%	-7.74%
Farm and Home Financial Corp.	Savings Institutions	$118,583	10.74%	28.71%	5.28%	-7.26%

Profitable Growers (continued)

Company Name	Fortune Industry	Company Size Revenue 93 (000s)	88-93 Company Revenue Growth	88-93 Company Operating Profit Growth	88-93 Industry Revenue Growth	88-93 Industry Operating Profit Growth
Federal Home Loan Mortgage Corp.	Diversified Financial	$5,456,000	13.73%	39.22%	2.73%	7.24%
Federal National Mortgage Association	Diversified Financial	$16,053,000	8.58%	35.29%	2.73%	7.24%
Federal-Mogul Corp.	Motor Vehicles and Parts	$1,575,500	6.01%	-1.36%	2.73%	-4.44%
Federated Department Stores Inc.	Retailing	$7,229,400	15.15%	18.44%	7.22%	5.59%
Ferro Corp.	Chemicals	$1,065,700	1.10%	0.19%	-0.40%	-8.42%
FHP International Corp.	Diversified Services	$2,005,900	31.84%	15.43%	7.95%	0.19%
Fifth Third Bancorp	Commercial Banking	$662,967	18.85%	21.33%	10.69%	15.00%
First Alabama Bancshares Inc.	Commercial Banking	$474,080	13.30%	16.90%	10.69%	15.00%
First Bank System Inc.	Commercial Banking	$1,702,500	35.96%	120.24%	10.69%	15.00%
First Citizens Bancshares Inc.	Commercial Banking	$312,684	13.02%	21.90%	10.69%	15.00%
First Commerce Corp.	Commercial Banking	$352,431	12.06%	34.79%	10.69%	15.00%
First Data Corp.	Diversified Services	$1,490,300	26.18%	9.29%	7.95%	0.19%
First Empire State Corp.	Commercial Banking	$581,300	20.34%	21.68%	10.69%	15.00%
First Financial Corp.	Savings Institutions	$188,110	13.52%	34.16%	5.28%	-7.26%
First Financial Management Corp.	Diversified Services	$1,659,800	31.86%	33.53%	7.95%	0.19%
First Maryland Bancorp	Commercial Banking	$616,644	11.84%	19.69%	10.69%	15.00%
First of America Bank Corp.	Commercial Banking	$1,194,201	20.88%	23.58%	10.69%	15.00%
First Security Corp.	Commercial Banking	$571,097	17.27%	33.56%	10.69%	15.00%
First Tennessee National Corp.	Commercial Banking	$617,043	13.68%	23.58%	10.69%	15.00%
First Union Corp.	Commercial Banking	$3,964,181	21.72%	36.43%	10.69%	15.00%
Fleet Financial Group Inc.	Commercial Banking	$3,516,000	40.65%	34.38%	10.69%	15.00%
Fleetwood Enterprises Inc.	Motor Vehicles and Parts	$1,941,900	3.71%	0.44%	2.73%	-4.44%
Fluor Corp.	Diversified Services	$7,971,200	9.20%	21.74%	7.95%	0.19%
FMC Corp.	Chemicals	$3,753,900	2.69%	-3.93%	-0.40%	-8.42%
Fort Howard Corp.	Forest and Paper Products	$1,187,400	10.40%	23.83%	3.87%	-10.32%
Foster Wheeler Corp.	Diversified Services	$2,583,000	19.64%	22.09%	7.95%	0.19%
Foundation Health Corp.	Diversified Services	$1,517,339	42.42%	128.64%	7.95%	0.19%
Fourth Financial Corp.	Commercial Banking	$347,069	21.43%	24.34%	10.69%	15.00%
Fred Meyer Inc.	Retailing	$2,979,100	7.52%	14.23%	7.22%	5.59%
Fremont General Corp.	Diversified Financial	$651,405	9.83%	15.87%	2.73%	7.24%

Profitable Growers (continued)

Company Name	Fortune Industry	Company Size Revenue 93 (000s)	88-93 Company Revenue Growth	88-93 Company Operating Profit Growth	88-93 Industry Revenue Growth	88-93 Industry Operating Profit Growth
Fruit of the Loom Inc.	Apparel	$1,884,400	13.40%	12.56%	9.09%	12.56%
The GAP Inc.	Retailing	$3,295,700	21.36%	26.92%	7.22%	5.59%
GATX Corp.	Transportation	$1,086,900	13.11%	3.63%	7.64%	0.69%
Geico Corp.	Diversified Financial	$2,638,300	8.61%	18.19%	2.73%	7.24%
General Mills Inc.	Food	$8,134,600	10.31%	12.69%	7.38%	9.42%
General Public Utilities Corp.	Utilities	$3,596,100	4.88%	4.43%	3.89%	3.98%
General Re Corp.	Diversified Financial	$3,560,200	5.46%	9.44%	2.73%	7.24%
Genuine Parts Co.	Diversified Services	$4,384,300	8.31%	7.95%	7.95%	0.19%
Giddings and Lewis Inc.	Industrial and Farm Equipment	$517,462	25.09%	54.85%	4.51%	7.25%
Gillette Co.	Metal Products	$5,410,800	8.60%	12.11%	7.06%	6.87%
Golden West Financial Corp.	Savings Institutions	$794,800	14.49%	15.68%	5.28%	-7.26%
Great Lakes Chemical Corp.	Chemicals	$1,792,000	24.30%	35.62%	-0.40%	-8.42%
H&R Block Inc.	Diversified Services	$1,525,330	13.80%	35.97%	7.95%	0.19%
H.B. Fuller Co.	Chemicals	$975,300	7.32%	5.08%	-0.40%	-8.42%
Handy and Harman	Metals	$658,253	0.00%	-4.12%	-1.18%	-29.36%
Harley-Davidson Inc.	Transportation Equipment	$1,217,400	9.96%	13.85%	0.19%	-6.33%
Harper Group Inc.	Transportation	$429,938	8.71%	2.24%	7.64%	0.69%
Harris Corp.	Electronics and Electrical Equipment	$3,099,100	11.50%	9.37%	5.09%	9.16%
Hercules Inc.	Chemicals	$2,773,400	-0.21%	24.93%	-0.40%	-8.42%
Hershey Foods Corp.	Food	$3,488,200	9.98%	11.44%	7.38%	9.42%
Hewlett Packard Co.	Computers and Office Equipment	$20,317,000	15.63%	10.47%	6.22%	-14.08%
Hillenbrand Industries Inc.	Metal Products	$1,447,900	10.36%	11.59%	7.06%	6.87%
Hoechst Celanese Corp.	Chemicals	$6,899,000	3.97%	-6.69%	-0.40%	-8.42%
Holly Corp.	Petroleum Refining	$629,884	10.34%	-5.53%	2.04%	-7.74%
Home Depot Inc.	Retailing	$9,238,763	35.81%	41.00%	7.22%	5.59%
Homestake Mining Co.	Mining and Crude Oil Production	$703,500	15.28%	171.11%	-1.19%	-14.59%
Hon Industries Inc.	Furniture	$780,300	7.94%	10.43%	5.49%	3.88%
Household International Inc.	Diversified Financial	$4,455,000	11.05%	9.05%	2.73%	7.24%
Hudson Foods Inc.	Food	$920,500	10.89%	48.24%	7.38%	9.42%
Huffy Corp.	Transportation Equipment	$757,900	17.69%	15.60%	0.19%	-6.33%

Profitable Growers (continued)

Company Name	Fortune Industry	Company Size Revenue 93 (000s)	88-93 Company Revenue Growth	88-93 Company Operating Profit Growth	88-93 Industry Revenue Growth	88-93 Industry Operating Profit Growth
Huntington Bancshares Inc.	Commercial Banking	$1,101,978	17.34%	23.66%	10.69%	15.00%
Illinois Tool Works Inc.	Metal Products	$3,159,200	10.36%	8.36%	7.06%	6.87%
Intel Corp.	Electronics and Electrical Equipment	$8,782,000	25.03%	41.67%	5.09%	9.16%
Intelligent Electronics Inc.	Diversified Services	$2,646,100	82.98%	53.52%	7.95%	0.19%
International Controls Corp.	Motor Vehicles and Parts	$909,300	10.91%	40.59%	2.73%	-4.44%
International Paper Co.	Forest and Paper Products	$13,685,000	7.50%	-9.56%	3.87%	-10.32%
International Shipholding Corp.	Transportation	$341,651	14.92%	8.69%	7.64%	0.69%
The Interpublic Group of Cos. Inc.	Diversified Services	$1,739,778	8.58%	15.46%	7.95%	0.19%
Ivax Corp.	Pharmaceuticals	$645,283	60.34%	271.97%	10.18%	3.55%
J B Hunt Transport Services Inc.	Transportation	$1,020,900	21.06%	5.65%	7.64%	0.69%
The J E Seagram Co. Ltd.	Beverages	$6,038,000	9.61%	21.42%	8.90%	12.23%
J P Morgan and Co. Inc.	Commercial Banking	$6,271,000	13.51%	15.41%	10.69%	15.00%
Jefferson Smurfit Corp.	Forest and Paper Products	$2,947,600	18.62%	-3.04%	3.87%	-10.32%
Johnson Controls Inc.	Scientific, Photographic, Control Equipment	$6,181,700	14.80%	7.24%	4.24%	2.91%
JPS Textile Group Inc.	Textiles	$885,700	16.77%	21.58%	-1.34%	3.62%
Kansas City Southern Industries Inc.	Transportation	$961,100	13.63%	28.82%	7.64%	0.69%
Kerr-McGee Corp.	Petroleum Refining	$3,281,000	4.06%	-5.91%	2.04%	-7.74%
Keycorp	Commercial Banking	$1,971,909	21.47%	28.42%	10.69%	15.00%
Kimberly-Clark Corp.	Forest and Paper Products	$6,972,900	5.27%	4.37%	3.87%	-10.32%
Knight-Ridder Inc.	Publishing and Printing	$2,451,300	3.60%	3.40%	3.51%	0.48%
Lear Seating Corp.	Furniture	$1,756,510	16.82%	11.04%	5.49%	3.88%
Leggett and Platt Inc.	Furniture	$1,526,700	13.52%	18.51%	5.49%	3.88%
Leucadia National Corp.	Diversified Financial	$1,408,100	9.37%	35.39%	2.73%	7.24%
Levi Strauss Associates Inc.	Apparel	$5,892,500	13.58%	16.72%	9.09%	12.56%
Liberty National Bancorp Inc.	Commercial Banking	$251,476	12.61%	15.20%	10.69%	15.00%
The Limited Inc.	Retailing	$7,245,088	12.22%	8.38%	7.22%	5.59%
Lincoln National Life Insurance Co.	Life Insurance	$7,389,600	27.72%	29.51%	7.03%	7.02%
Liz Claiborne Inc.	Diversified Services	$2,204,300	13.23%	1.39%	7.95%	0.19%
Loctite Corp.	Chemicals	$612,600	6.06%	3.84%	-0.40%	-8.42%
Long Island Lighting Co.	Utilities	$2,881,000	6.15%	7.86%	3.89%	3.98%

Profitable Growers (continued)

Company Name	Fortune Industry	Company Size Revenue 93 (000s)	88-93 Company Revenue Growth	88-93 Company Operating Profit Growth	88-93 Industry Revenue Growth	88-93 Industry Operating Profit Growth
Loral Corp.	Electronics and Electrical Equipment	$4,008,700	27.56%	24.76%	5.09%	9.16%
Lotus Development Corp.	Computers and Office Equipment	$981,168	15.93%	11.54%	6.22%	-14.08%
Louisiana Land and Exploration Co.	Mining and Crude Oil Production	$815,400	3.24%	130.92%	-1.19%	-14.59%
Louisiana Pacific Corp.	Forest and Paper Products	$2,511,300	6.89%	10.84%	3.87%	-10.32%
Lowes Cos. Inc.	Retailing	$4,538,000	12.51%	14.99%	7.22%	5.59%
LSI Logic Corp.	Electronics and Electrical Equipment	$718,800	13.66%	26.26%	5.09%	9.16%
The Lubrizol Corp.	Chemicals	$1,517,600	6.31%	7.63%	-0.40%	-8.42%
Lukens Inc.	Metals	$1,033,300	11.29%	-3.11%	-1.18%	-29.36%
M.A. Hanna Co.	Rubber and Plastic Products	$1,560,800	8.90%	9.82%	3.61%	7.04%
Magna Group Inc.	Commercial Banking	$191,103	14.64%	20.72%	10.69%	15.00%
Mallinckrodt Group Inc.	Chemicals	$1,796,300	14.84%	48.36%	-0.40%	-8.42%
Mapco Inc.	Petroleum Refining	$2,715,300	8.54%	5.96%	2.04%	-7.74%
Mark IV Industries Inc.	Rubber and Plastic Products	$1,222,000	10.48%	10.87%	3.61%	7.04%
Martin Marietta Corp.	Aerospace	$9,435,700	45.98%	42.01%	2.85%	6.21%
Massachusetts Mutual Life Insurance Co.	Life Insurance	$7,037,000	8.99%	11.41%	7.03%	7.02%
Mattel Inc.	Toys and Sporting Goods	$2,704,400	22.26%	33.70%	18.81%	23.39%
Maxus Energy Corp.	Mining and Crude Oil Production	$786,700	6.47%	131.97%	-1.19%	-14.59%
MBIA Inc.	Diversified Financial	$429,000	23.28%	24.32%	2.73%	7.24%
MBNA Corp.	Commercial Banking	$1,214,291	24.59%	19.92%	10.69%	15.00%
McCaw Cellular Communications Inc.	Telecommunications	$2,194,800	47.83%	134.74%	7.59%	11.38%
McGraw-Hill Inc.	Publishing and Printing	$2,195,500	3.85%	1.31%	3.51%	0.48%
MCI Communications Corp.	Telecommunications	$11,921,000	18.34%	16.77%	7.59%	11.38%
McKesson Corp.	Diversified Services	$11,672,200	10.62%	5.51%	7.95%	0.19%
Medco Containment Services Inc.	Diversified Services	$2,624,000	39.17%	48.49%	7.95%	0.19%
Medtronic Inc.	Scientific, Photographic, Control Equipment	$1,328,200	12.36%	17.88%	4.24%	2.91%
Mercantile Bancorporation Inc.	Commercial Banking	$620,818	14.60%	103.63%	10.69%	15.00%
Merck and Co. Inc.	Pharmaceuticals	$10,498,200	12.07%	15.96%	10.18%	3.55%
Meridian Bancorp Inc.	Commercial Banking	$902,562	12.20%	15.93%	10.69%	15.00%
Merisel Inc.	Diversified Services	$3,085,900	46.01%	34.27%	7.95%	0.19%
Mesa Airlines Inc.	Transportation	$353,640	82.41%	62.00%	7.64%	0.69%

Company Name	Fortune Industry	Company Size Revenue 93 (000s)	88-93 Company Revenue Growth	88-93 Company Operating Profit Growth	88-93 Industry Revenue Growth	88-93 Industry Operating Profit Growth
Metropolitan Financial Corp.	Savings Institutions	$287,951	31.00%	53.20%	5.28%	-7.26%
Microage Inc.	Diversified Services	$1,509,823	42.77%	21.79%	7.95%	0.19%
Microsoft Corp.	Computers and Office Equipment	$3,753,000	44.74%	47.89%	6.22%	-14.08%
Mitchell Energy and Development Corp.	Mining and Crude Oil Production	$952,809	10.54%	17.48%	-1.19%	-14.59%
MNX Inc.	Transportation	$441,100	38.93%	2.19%	7.64%	0.69%
Morgan Stanley Group Inc.	Diversified Financial	$9,176,000	17.43%	13.52%	2.73%	7.24%
Morton International Inc.	Chemicals	$2,330,900	13.30%	8.30%	-0.40%	-8.42%
Motorola Inc.	Electronics and Electrical Equipment	$16,963,000	15.51%	18.60%	5.09%	9.16%
Murphy Oil Corp.	Petroleum Refining	$1,636,700	2.12%	4.86%	2.04%	-7.74%
Nacco Industries Inc.	Industrial and Farm Equipment	$1,549,400	20.24%	9.02%	4.51%	7.25%
Nalco Chemical Co.	Chemicals	$1,389,400	6.92%	10.59%	-0.40%	-8.42%
National Semiconductor Corp.	Electronics and Electrical Equipment	$2,013,700	7.05%	112.30%	5.09%	9.16%
Nationsbank Corp.	Commercial Banking	$6,822,000	14.80%	18.31%	10.69%	15.00%
Nationwide Life Insurance Co.	Life Insurance	$5,524,000	17.98%	16.95%	7.03%	7.02%
Navistar International Corp.	Motor Vehicles and Parts	$4,694,000	2.84%	25.13%	2.73%	-4.44%
NBB Bancorp Inc.	Savings Institutions	$107,939	22.47%	19.78%	5.28%	-7.26%
NBD Bancorp Inc.	Commercial Banking	$2,143,490	16.41%	21.54%	10.69%	15.00%
Newell Co.	Metal Products	$1,645,000	10.73%	18.15%	7.06%	6.87%
Newmont Mining Corp.	Mining and Crude Oil Production	$634,300	4.87%	-9.42%	-1.19%	-14.59%
Nike Inc.	Diversified Services	$3,931,000	26.71%	32.29%	7.95%	0.19%
Northeast Utilities	Utilities	$3,629,100	11.78%	12.23%	3.89%	3.98%
Northwest Airlines Inc.	Transportation	$8,648,900	9.25%	6.31%	7.64%	0.69%
Northwestern Mutual Life Insurance Co.	Life Insurance	$8,777,500	8.89%	10.05%	7.03%	7.02%
Norwest Corp.	Commercial Banking	$3,918,600	24.31%	35.32%	10.69%	15.00%
Novell Inc.	Computers and Office Equipment	$1,122,896	31.91%	53.33%	6.22%	-14.08%
Nucor Corp.	Metals	$2,253,700	16.25%	12.71%	-1.18%	-29.36%
Ogden Corp.	Diversified Services	$2,039,300	13.39%	34.52%	7.95%	0.19%
Old Republic International Corp.	Diversified Financial	$1,736,300	9.52%	31.02%	2.73%	7.24%
Olsten Corp.	Diversified Services	$2,157,535	33.13%	29.33%	7.95%	0.19%
Omnicom Group Inc.	Diversified Services	$1,516,500	11.47%	14.86%	7.95%	0.19%

Profitable Growers (continued)

Company Name	Fortune Industry	Company Size Revenue 93 (000s)	88-93 Company Revenue Growth	88-93 Company Operating Profit Growth	88-93 Industry Revenue Growth	88-93 Industry Operating Profit Growth
Oracle Systems Corp.	Diversified Services	$1,502,768	20.82%	12.03%	7.95%	0.19%
Oregon Steel Mills Inc.	Metals	$679,823	29.00%	-8.58%	-1.18%	-29.36%
Oryx Energy Co.	Mining and Crude Oil Production	$1,080,000	0.19%	110.20%	-1.19%	-14.59%
Pacific Gas and Electric Co.	Utilities	$10,582,400	6.72%	10.39%	3.89%	3.98%
Pacific Mutual Life Insurance Co.	Life Insurance	$3,210,100	9.61%	23.15%	7.03%	7.02%
Pacificare Health Systems Inc.	Diversified Services	$2,200,200	38.94%	90.14%	7.95%	0.19%
PaineWebber Group Inc.	Diversified Financial	$4,004,700	9.77%	45.17%	2.73%	7.24%
Pall Corp.	Scientific, Photographic, Control Equipment	$687,200	9.29%	9.58%	4.24%	2.91%
Panhandle Eastern Corp.	Utilities	$2,120,900	10.95%	38.66%	3.89%	3.98%
Payless Cashways Inc.	Retailing	$2,601,003	32.48%	36.13%	7.22%	5.59%
PECO Energy Co.	Utilities	$3,988,100	4.32%	6.45%	3.89%	3.98%
Penn Traffic Co.	Retailing	$3,171,600	21.87%	41.09%	7.22%	5.59%
Pennzoil Co.	Petroleum Refining	$2,742,200	5.60%	-6.69%	2.04%	-7.74%
People's Bank	Savings Institutions	$337,553	10.16%	-3.86%	5.28%	-7.26%
Pepsico Inc.	Beverages	$25,020,700	13.98%	18.74%	8.90%	12.23%
Perkin-Elmer Corp.	Scientific, Photographic, Control Equipment	$1,118,000	10.33%	6.29%	4.24%	2.91%
Phelps Dodge Corp.	Metals	$2,611,100	2.39%	-12.20%	-1.18%	-29.36%
Philip Morris Cos. Inc.	Food	$50,621,000	9.78%	12.52%	7.38%	9.42%
Phoenix Home Life Mutual Insurance Co.	Life Insurance	$1,892,500	7.46%	11.50%	7.03%	7.02%
Pilgrim's Pride Corp.	Food	$887,800	11.88%	220.51%	7.38%	9.42%
Pioneer Hi-Bred International Inc.	Diversified Services	$1,343,437	8.96%	13.43%	7.95%	0.19%
Ply-Gem Industries Inc.	Forest and Paper Products	$722,660	13.50%	5.00%	3.87%	-10.32%
Pope and Talbot Inc.	Forest and Paper Products	$628,926	4.08%	-3.05%	3.87%	-10.32%
PPG Industries Inc.	Chemicals	$5,753,900	0.48%	-4.42%	-0.40%	-8.42%
Price Co.	Retailing	$7,821,700	14.05%	29.44%	7.22%	5.59%
Principal Mutual Life Insurance Co.	Life Insurance	$12,370,200	12.65%	13.33%	7.03%	7.02%
Procter and Gamble Co.	Soaps and Cosmetics	$30,433,000	9.50%	11.97%	9.01%	10.89%
The Progressive Corp.	Diversified Financial	$1,954,800	9.76%	68.59%	2.73%	7.24%
Public Service Enterprise Group Inc.	Utilities	$5,705,600	5.36%	7.43%	3.89%	3.98%
Publix Super Markets Inc.	Retailing	$7,472,700	9.21%	11.15%	7.22%	5.59%

Company Name	Fortune Industry	Company Size Revenue 93 (000s)	88-93 Company Revenue Growth	88-93 Company Operating Profit Growth	88-93 Industry Revenue Growth	88-93 Industry Operating Profit Growth
Quanex Corp.	Metals	$616,145	5.89%	-14.19%	-1.18%	-29.36%
Quantum Corp.	Computers and Office Equipment	$2,131,054	59.26%	21.63%	6.22%	-14.08%
R.R. Donnelley and Sons Co.	Publishing and Printing	$4,387,800	8.80%	5.83%	3.51%	0.48%
The Readers Digest Association Inc.	Publishing and Printing	$2,868,600	10.88%	10.57%	3.51%	0.48%
Reebok International Ltd.	Diversified Services	$2,893,900	10.13%	11.05%	7.95%	0.19%
Richfood Holdings Inc.	Diversified Services	$1,091,438	32.51%	39.82%	7.95%	0.19%
Roadway Services Inc.	Transportation	$4,155,900	13.73%	15.08%	7.64%	0.69%
Rohm and Haas Co.	Chemicals	$3,269,000	5.22%	-3.15%	-0.40%	-8.42%
Roosevelt Financial Group Inc.	Savings Institutions	$94,528	11.41%	16.86%	5.28%	-7.26%
RPM Inc.	Chemicals	$625,680	10.71%	14.24%	-0.40%	-8.42%
Rubbermaid Inc.	Rubber and Plastic Products	$1,960,200	10.43%	15.11%	3.61%	7.04%
Safeco Corp.	Diversified Financial	$3,516,700	4.13%	14.06%	2.73%	7.24%
Salomon Inc.	Diversified Financial	$8,799,000	7.44%	14.24%	2.73%	7.24%
SCI Systems Inc.	Computers and Office Equipment	$1,697,100	17.00%	7.87%	6.22%	-14.08%
Seagate Technology Inc.	Computers and Office Equipment	$3,043,600	19.18%	24.21%	6.22%	-14.08%
Shaw Industries Inc.	Textiles	$2,320,800	19.35%	21.10%	-1.34%	3.62%
Sherwin-Williams Co.	Chemicals	$2,949,300	8.62%	14.95%	-0.40%	-8.42%
Sigma Aldrich Corp.	Chemicals	$739,400	14.53%	13.35%	-0.40%	-8.42%
Silicon Graphics Inc.	Computers and Office Equipment	$1,091,200	32.84%	53.64%	6.22%	-14.08%
Smith's Food and Drug Centers Inc.	Retailing	$2,807,165	15.04%	18.45%	7.22%	5.59%
Society Corp.	Commercial Banking	$1,708,774	27.56%	32.69%	10.69%	15.00%
Solectron Corp.	Electronics and Electrical Equipment	$836,326	69.51%	53.45%	5.09%	9.16%
Sonoco Products Co.	Forest and Paper Products	$1,947,200	4.01%	2.53%	3.87%	-10.32%
Southern National Corp.	Commercial Banking	$290,939	18.73%	31.17%	10.69%	15.00%
Southtrust Corp.	Commercial Banking	$704,510	20.17%	21.94%	10.69%	15.00%
Southwest Airlines Co.	Transportation	$2,296,700	21.70%	28.63%	7.64%	0.69%
Sovereign Bancorp Inc.	Savings Institutions	$129,852	40.79%	45.06%	5.28%	-7.26%
Sprint Corp.	Telecommunications	$11,367,800	11.85%	46.53%	7.59%	11.38%
St. Paul Bancorp Inc.	Savings Institutions	$156,461	10.48%	9.88%	5.28%	-7.26%
Standard Federal Bank	Savings Institutions	$342,596	11.49%	14.31%	5.28%	-7.26%

Profitable Growers (continued)

Company Name	Fortune Industry	Company Size Revenue 93 (000s)	88-93 Company Revenue Growth	88-93 Company Operating Profit Growth	88-93 Industry Revenue Growth	88-93 Industry Operating Profit Growth
Stewart and Stevenson Services Inc.	Industrial and Farm Equipment	$981,892	15.70%	21.06%	4.51%	7.25%
Sun Microsystems Inc.	Computers and Office Equipment	$4,308,600	32.59%	16.71%	6.22%	-14.08%
Synoptics Communications Inc.	Electronics and Electrical Equipment	$704,493	77.40%	74.51%	5.09%	9.16%
Synovus Financial Corp.	Commercial Banking	$455,149	23.36%	26.64%	10.69%	15.00%
Sysco Corp.	Diversified Services	$10,021,500	17.98%	20.71%	7.95%	0.19%
TCF Financial Corp.	Savings Institutions	$304,039	10.13%	24.14%	5.28%	-7.26%
Tech Data Corp.	Diversified Services	$1,532,352	44.09%	31.49%	7.95%	0.19%
Tejas Gas Corp.	Transportation	$790,178	29.04%	23.44%	7.64%	0.69%
Tele-Communications Inc.	Telecommunications	$4,153,000	12.72%	13.31%	7.59%	11.38%
Teleflex Inc.	Industrial and Farm Equipment	$666,796	15.56%	11.95%	4.51%	7.25%
Temple-Inland Inc.	Forest and Paper Products	$2,735,900	9.06%	153.91%	3.87%	-10.32%
Tenneco Inc.	Industrial and Farm Equipment	$13,255,000	6.90%	43.96%	4.51%	7.25%
Texas Industries Inc.	Metals	$614,300	-0.67%	-10.09%	-1.18%	-29.36%
Texas Instruments Inc.	Electronics and Electrical Equipment	$8,523,000	6.25%	9.61%	5.09%	9.16%
Texas Utilities Co.	Utilities	$5,434,500	5.52%	6.87%	3.89%	3.98%
Thermo Electron Corp.	Scientific, Photographic, Control Equipment	$1,249,700	21.58%	168.01%	4.24%	2.91%
TJX Cos. Inc.	Retailing	$3,626,600	13.55%	9.51%	7.22%	5.59%
Tosco Corp.	Petroleum Refining	$3,559,200	25.52%	11.34%	2.04%	-7.74%
Toys R Us Inc.	Retailing	$7,946,100	14.71%	13.14%	7.22%	5.59%
Transatlantic Holdings Inc.	Diversified Financial	$720,000	7.48%	12.41%	2.73%	7.24%
Trinity Industries Inc.	Transportation Equipment	$1,540,000	8.99%	9.38%	0.19%	-6.33%
Turner Broadcasting System Inc.	Diversified Services	$1,921,600	18.96%	6.47%	7.95%	0.19%
The Turner Corp.	Diversified Services	$2,768,400	111.25%	2.38%	7.95%	0.19%
Tyson Foods Inc.	Food	$4,707,400	19.45%	26.67%	7.38%	9.42%
U S Healthcare Inc.	Diversified Services	$2,559,700	28.70%	255.97%	7.95%	0.19%
U.S. Bancorp	Commercial Banking	$1,459,930	14.40%	18.70%	10.69%	15.00%
Unifi Inc.	Textiles	$1,332,200	34.89%	45.06%	-1.34%	3.62%
Union Planters Corp.	Commercial Banking	$319,404	12.31%	19.96%	10.69%	15.00%
Uniroyal Chemical Co. Inc.	Chemicals	$907,862	4.34%	5.86%	-0.40%	-8.42%
United Healthcare Corp.	Diversified Services	$2,469,400	41.21%	277.42%	7.95%	0.19%

Profitable Growers (continued)

Company Name	Fortune Industry	Company Size Revenue 93 (000s)	88-93 Company Revenue Growth	88-93 Company Operating Profit Growth	88-93 Industry Revenue Growth	88-93 Industry Operating Profit Growth
United Parcel Service of America Inc.	Transportation	$17,782,400	10.02%	6.87%	7.64%	0.69%
United Stationers Inc.	Diversified Services	$1,470,115	11.42%	1.77%	7.95%	0.19%
Universal Corp.	Tobacco	$3,047,200	0.85%	9.31%	-2.42%	2.23%
Unum Life Insurance Co. of America	Life Insurance	$2,756,200	23.05%	25.58%	7.03%	7.02%
UST Inc.	Tobacco	$1,076,100	11.71%	16.76%	-2.42%	2.23%
Valero Energy Corp.	Petroleum Refining	$1,222,200	9.66%	14.29%	2.04%	-7.74%
Valspar Corp.	Chemicals	$693,700	7.66%	15.99%	-0.40%	-8.42%
Variable Annuity Life Insurance Co.	Life Insurance	$3,659,500	13.25%	44.07%	7.03%	7.02%
Viacom Inc.	Diversified Services	$2,004,900	9.76%	19.25%	7.95%	0.19%
Vigoro Corp.	Chemicals	$578,232	6.52%	39.49%	-0.40%	-8.42%
Vishay Intertechnology Inc.	Electronics and Electrical Equipment	$856,300	37.25%	29.81%	5.09%	9.16%
Vulcan Materials Co.	Mining and Crude Oil Production	$1,133,500	1.48%	-8.92%	-1.19%	-14.59%
W. R. Grace and Co.	Chemicals	$5,736,600	-0.17%	-7.78%	-0.40%	-8.42%
W. W. Grainger Inc.	Diversified Services	$2,628,400	11.35%	7.23%	7.95%	0.19%
Waban Inc.	Retailing	$3,589,300	16.78%	13.64%	7.22%	5.59%
Wachovia Corp.	Commercial Banking	$1,903,398	13.00%	16.97%	10.69%	15.00%
Wal-Mart Stores Inc.	Retailing	$67,344,600	26.66%	21.68%	7.22%	5.59%
Walgreen Co.	Retailing	$8,294,800	11.18%	12.62%	7.22%	5.59%
The Walt Disney Co.	Diversified Services	$8,529,200	19.93%	14.62%	7.95%	0.19%
Washington Federal Savings and Loan	Savings Institutions	$172,185	12.69%	13.28%	5.28%	-7.26%
Wellman Inc.	Chemicals	$842,100	21.76%	4.78%	-0.40%	-8.42%
Werner Enterprises Inc.	Transportation	$432,658	17.71%	13.35%	7.64%	0.69%
West One Bancorp	Commercial Banking	$406,399	16.97%	24.55%	10.69%	15.00%
Westcorp	Savings Institutions	$130,582	12.41%	3.11%	5.28%	-7.26%
Weyerhaeuser Co.	Forest and Paper Products	$9,544,800	3.95%	1.56%	3.87%	-10.32%
Wheeling-Pittsburgh Steel Corp.	Metals	$1,046,800	-1.04%	-22.37%	-1.18%	-29.36%
Whirlpool Corp.	Electronics and Electrical Equipment	$7,533,000	11.25%	15.51%	5.09%	9.16%
Willamette Industries Inc.	Forest and Paper Products	$2,622,200	8.85%	-2.02%	3.87%	-10.32%
The Williams Companies Inc.	Telecommunications	$2,438,200	7.82%	14.19%	7.59%	11.38%
Witco Corp.	Chemicals	$2,142,600	6.20%	4.77%	-0.40%	-8.42%

Profitable Growers (continued)

Company Name	Fortune Industry	Company Size Revenue 93 (000s)	88-93 Company Revenue Growth	88-93 Company Operating Profit Growth	88-93 Industry Revenue Growth	88-93 Industry Operating Profit Growth
Wlr Foods Inc.	Food	$616,702	10.09%	26.26%	7.38%	9.42%
Wm. Wrigley Jr. Co.	Food	$1,428,500	9.89%	15.42%	7.38%	9.42%
WMX Technologies	Diversified Services	$9,135,600	20.70%	6.56%	7.95%	0.19%
Worthington Industries Inc.	Metals	$1,115,700	5.81%	0.35%	-1.18%	-29.36%
York International Corp.	Industrial and Farm Equipment	$2,031,900	16.10%	25.39%	4.51%	7.25%

Notes

INTRODUCTION

1. Myron Magnet, "Let's Go for Growth," *Fortune,* March 7, 1994, 60.
2. Mercer Management Consulting, executive survey, Nov. 1994.

CHAPTER 1: YOU CANNOT SHRINK TO GREATNESS

1. American Management Association (AMA), *1993 Survey on Downsizing,* 3.
2. Gregory H. Watson, *Strategic Benchmarking* (New York: John Wiley & Sons, Inc., 1993), 149–150.
3. William F. Glavin, "Competitive Benchmarking, A Technique Utilized by Xerox Corporation to Revitalize Itself to a Modern Competitive Position," *Review of Business* 6 (3), Winter 1984, 10.
4. CSC Index, "State of Reengineering Report," Cambridge, Mass., 1994, 26–27.
5. Ibid., 54.
6. Glenn Collins, "Tough Leader Wields the Ax at Scott," *New York Times,* August 15, 1994, section D, 1.
7. AMA, *1993 Survey on Downsizing.*
8. "When slimming is not enough," *The Economist,* Sept. 3, 1994, 59.

CHAPTER 2: SHATTERING THE MYTHS OF CORPORATE GROWTH

1. The "coefficient of correlation," or R-squared, for this data is 0.004—which indicates no correlation. An R-squared of +1.0 represents a perfect correlation; a −1.0 is a perfectly inverse correlation.
2. Charles Baden-Fuller and John M. Stopford, *Rejuvenating the Mature Business* (Boston: Harvard Business School Press, 1994), 113–114.
3. Zenas Block and Ian C. MacMillan, *Corporate Venturing* (Boston: Harvard Business School Press, 1993), 5.
4. Alfred D. Chandler, Jr., *Scale and Scope: The Dynamics of Industrial Capitalism* (Cambridge, Mass.: Harvard University Press, 1990).
5. Peter Lynch, "The Stock Market Hit Parade," *Worth,* July-August 1994, 32.
6. Baden-Fuller and Stopford, op. cit., 30.
7. Richard Rumelt, "How Much Does Industry Matter?" *Strategic Management Journal,* March 12, 1991, 167–186.
8. Robert D. Buzzell and Bradley T. Gale, *The PIMS Principles (Profit Impact of Market Strategy): Linking Strategy to Performance* (New York: The Free Press, 1987), 56.
9. Tom Copeland, Tim Roller, and Jack Murrin, *Valuation Measuring and Managing the Value of Companies* (New York: John Wiley & Sons, Inc., 1993), 416.
10. Ibid.

Notes

11. Michael T. Jacobs, *Short Term America:* (Boston: Harvard Business School Press, 1991), 20.

12. "Primerica: Sandy Weill and His Corporate Entrepreneurs," Harvard Business School, Case Study 9-393–040, Nov. 20, 1992, 2.

13. Ibid., 5.

14. Ibid., 14.

CHAPTER 5: NEW PRODUCT AND SERVICE DEVELOPMENT

1. Alan Deutschman, "How H-P Continues to Grow and Grow," *Fortune,* May 2, 1994, 90.

2. Lawrence M. Fisher, "A PC Elitist Turns Crowd Pleaser," *New York Times,* Feb. 12, 1995, 6.

3. George Stalk and Thomas Hout, *Competing Against Time: How Time-Based Competition Is Reshaping Global Markets* (New York: The Free Press, 1990), 58.

4. For full discussion of Hewlett-Packard's efforts to improve time to market, see Chapter 5 of Gregory H. Watson, *Strategic Benchmarking* (New York: John Wiley & Sons, Inc., 1993), 93–107.

5. Rhonda L. Rundle, "Amgen Turns Bullish on Possible Lab Breakthroughs," *Wall Street Journal,* March 1995, B1.

CHAPTER 6: CHANNEL MANAGEMENT

1. Scott McCartney, "Dell Computer to Outsource All Shipping," *Wall Street Journal,* Feb. 15, 1995, B6.

2. *Chicago Tribune,* April 9, 1995, section 7, 2.

3. Joseph Radigan, "Look Out Home Banker—Here Comes William the Conqueror," *US Banker,* Dec. 1994, 22–27.

4. *Forbes,* April 24, 1995, 126.

5. As long ago as 1990, the fully loaded cost of face-to-face selling time was estimated at $500 per hour for a national account manager and roughly $300 per hour for direct sales representatives. See Rowland T. Moriarty and Ursala Moran, "Managing Hybrid Marketing Systems," *Harvard Business Review,* Nov.-Dec. 1990, 147.

6. CPAs are not allowed to receive financial compensation for referring their clients to a vendor.

7. Michael Barrier, "Tom Stemberg Calls the Office," *Nation's Business,* July 1990, p. 42.

CHAPTER 7: GROWTH FOUNDATIONS

1. Bradley T. Gale, *Managing Customer Value* (New York: The Free Press, 1994), 26.

2. Jean-Philippe Deschamps and P. Ranganath Nayak, *Product Juggernauts* (Boston: Harvard Business School Press, 1995), 00.

3. McDonald's Corp., "Getting Value for Your Money," *1993 Annual Report,* 4.

4. Strategic Choice Analysis®, whose roots are in psychology, econometrics,

Notes

and market research, first appeared in the late 1980s, and may be known to some readers as "discrete choice theory."

5. Richard Preston, *American Steel* (New York: Prentice Hall Press, 1991), 91–94.

6. James M. Utterback, *Mastering the Dynamics of Innovation* (Boston: Harvard Business School Press, 1994), 106–116.

7. John Enos, *Petroleum, Progress, and Profits: A History of Process Innovation* (Cambridge, Mass.: MIT Press, 1962), 131.

8. John J. Morse and Jay W. Lorsch, "Beyond Theory Y," *Harvard Business Review,* May–June 1970, 61.

9. Ibid., 62.

CHAPTER 8: GETTING TO GROWTH

1. Quoted in *Corning Glass Works: International (A),* Harvard Business School Case 9-3-79-051 (Boston: Harvard Business School, 1978).

2. Ira C. Magaziner and Mark Patinkin, *The Silent War* (New York: Random House, 1989), 276.

3. Keith H. Hammonds, "Corning's Class Act: How Jamie Houghton Reinvented the Company," *Business Week,* May 13, 1991, 70.

4. Joseph Rebello, "Cabot Corp.'s 'Soot' Turns to Gold Amid Demand Surge," *Wall Street Journal,* Feb. 14, 1995, B4.

5. Ibid.

6. See Julie Pitta, "It Had To Be Done," *Forbes,* April 26, 1993, 143–152.

7. Ibid., 151.

8. Lawrence M. Fisher, "A PC Elitist Turns Crowd Pleaser," *New York Times,* Feb. 12, 1995, 6.

9. Charles R. Day, Jr., "Shape Up and Ship Out," *Industry Week,* Feb. 6, 1995, 19.

10. See "The Wizard is Oz," *Chief Executive,* March 1994, 40–44.

11. Charles R. Day, Jr., op. cit., 17.

12. Ibid.

Index

About The Authors

Dwight L. Gertz is a vice president in the General Management Consulting Practice at Mercer Management Consulting. He lives in Lincoln, Massachusetts. João P. A. Baptista is a vice president in Mercer Management Consulting's London office, and heads Mercer's Telecommunications Practice in Europe.

The Gro

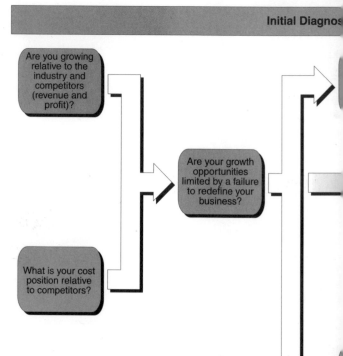